The Politics of Economic Regulation in Nigeria

Adonis & Abbey Publishers Ltd

St James House
13 Kensington Square,
London, W8 5HD
United Kingdom

Website: http://www.adonis-abbey.com
E-mail Address: editor@adonis-abbey.com

Nigeria:
Suites C4 – C6 J-Plus Plaza
Asokoro, Abuja, Nigeria
Tel: +234 (0) 7058078841/08052035034

British Library Cataloguing-in-Publication Data
A catalogue record for this book is available from the British Library

ISBN: 9781906704926

The Politics of Economic Regulation in Nigeria

Amaechi Anakwue

Acknowledgement

I wish to thank God almighty for giving me the wisdom, courage and perseverance to carry out this work.

My appreciation also goes to the members of the Anakwue family for their encouragement and support throughout my educational pursuit. Ngozi, Amaka, Nkemdili, Omunuzuo and Ujunnwa, you are always in my memory.

I am also full of appreciation to the founder, high chief Raymond Dopkesi, board, management and staff of DAAR Communications PLC, for giving me the opportunity to practice Journalism and be able to influence government programmes and policies, as well as shape public opinion. I am indeed very appreciative of the support and encouragement many of my colleagues provided in the course of this work.

I also have words of appreciation to a whole lot of people that helped in no small way in the success of this book, either by technical advice, research assistance and granting of interviews. They include, but not limited to the following:

Dr Hussani Tukur who painstakingly went through the entire work and made very useful suggestions, Dr Abubakar Kari, Dr Ernest Ereke, Dr Donald Ofili, Dr Jideofor Adibe, who provided technical guidance, Chinedu Nwigwe and Patrick Ederaro of Infrastructure Concession Regulatory Commission, ICRC, Mrs Ikram Kamal of the Library Department of the Bureau of Public Enterprises, BPE, for facilitating and providing the much needed materials that formed part of this work, Mr Ezeako Odi and Mr Nwabueze Njoku who proof-read the manuscript. Also worthy of mention are Barrister Handel Okoli, Osaretin Iyare and Patience Idoko who provided invaluable contributions.

My appreciation goes to Mr Sam Nwaobasi and Mr Ikechukwu Eze for facilitating very important interviews. I am also full of commendations for former head of service, Engr. Ebere Okeke, former Secretary to the Government of the Federation, Pius Anyim, who gave me very insightful tips on the operational mechanisms of the federal bureaucracy. I also appreciate former president Goodluck Jonathan for important explanations on some of his policy choices concerning economic regulation and the management of the Nigerian economy during his tenure as president.

This book would not have been possible but for the valuable mentorship of several academics who were of immeasurable assistance in my academic development. They include my PhD theses supervisor and erudite scholar, Professor Kabir Mato, Professor Ali Zoaka, Professor Oshita Oshita and Professor Abubakar Suleiman.

I also wish to extend my gratitude to those that played a part in this research that I cannot mention personally. May God bless you all.

In the final analysis, I take credit for the contents of this book.

Dedication

To

My darling wife, Ifeyinwa, (Osodieme) and my children, Chinonso, Chuwkwuemeka and Chidike.

And.

To all patriots dedicated to the growth and development of the Nigerian State

Table of Contents

Chapter One
The Creation of the Nigerian Economy...11

Chapter Two
Theoretical Perspective..65

Chapter Three
Nature of Regulatory Institutions in Nigeria 71

Chapter Four
Regulatory Institutions as Fourth Arm of Government.............................91

Chapter Five
Ensuring a Productive Private Sector 105

Chapter Six
A Compendium of Regulatory Agencies in Nigeria...............................123

Bibliography 139

Appendices

Appendix A 137

Appendix B 146

Index...171

Forward

Examining the character of Nigeria's political economy is not an easy task. Being a dependent capitalist economy, its structure and politics are still largely externally propelled, the systems are weak and the difference between the private and public is relatively blurred. Some of the industries considered private, have public origin and still largely depend on the sustenance and even guarantee of the public. Conversely, the so-called public sector is either comatose or captured by private political and economic interests. This is the politics and dynamics that Dr Anakwue tries to scrutinize in this book. Considering the author's engagement in strategic public conversations, I am not surprised that he decided to courageously take on this murky terrain that is considered an exclusive preserve of policymakers, major private sector actors and their allies in the academia.

The economic crisis and adjustment in the early 1980s had a monumental impact on not only the structure of Nigerian economy, it significantly altered the character of the state and its governance of the economy. The IMF and World Bank inspired structural Adjustment Programme resulted to a shift from state-led development paradigm to a market-led economy. While these changes might have coincided with the changing dynamics of the global political economy, Nigeria, is a minor player in the world capitalist system, its market base is weak and governance structure historically authoritarian and militarist, while its socio-political structure is constrained ominously by economy of affection and clientelism. This deepened corruption and essentially undermine systems and processes associated with efficient private sector regulation.

In the last two decades, I have been involved with politics of privatization, as a scholar, critic and policy advocate. While recognizing the importance of the private sector in the developing economies like Nigeria, I found its opportunistic, parasitic, dependent and unaccountable character inimical to the development imperatives and aspirations of the country. As the state withdraws from public service provision through different privatization mechanisms, strengthening private sector governance has become an important mechanism for deepening accountability and protecting consumers. Working with the government and the private sector to strengthen regulatory system can therefore be interesting and challenging. While they are both happy to have a framework, none want to be held to account.

The importance of this book is varied, depending on the interest of the reader. Dr Anakwue has taken us through an interesting history and operational dynamics of privatization and regulatory institutions. Nigeria has in the last three decades gone through a massive privatization effort despite resistance from popular groups including the labour unions and students' movement. This resistance was met with massive repressive and manipulative powers of the state. One important conversation in this interesting work is the challenge of regulatory capture – a systematic governance failure occasioned by poor regulatory performance, as regulatory agencies failed to act in public interest, but in the interest of those they are supposed to be regulating. This is an important challenge this book tries to unravel. The book is therefore rich in excellent details of different regulatory agencies including those that have collapsed under the weight of the government and the industries they are supposed to regulate.

Dr Anakwue has surely written a fascinating, nuanced and insightful book. He has demonstrated a strong understanding of this subject matter. His understanding of politics of privatization is surely provocative as is his approach to regulatory system. His policy recommendations advance the need for a robust regulatory culture and institutions that are independent of both the state and the private sector. The author identified these regulatory agencies as significant component of economic governance framework and constitute the fourth organ of government. The book is a significant contribution to the political economy of Nigeria, particularly the politics of privatization and regulatory agencies. I am therefore pleased to recommend this book to policymakers, private sector actors, academics and anybody interested in contemporary political economy of Nigeria.

Hussaini Abdu, PhD.
Country Director Plan International Nigeria,

CHAPTER ONE

The Creation of the Nigerian Economy

It will be pertinent to carry out a historical analysis of the place and role of governments, groups and individuals in the economy of Nigeria right from the medieval period. This will elucidate the nature and patterns of relations within the different economic systems, and in so doing, establish the levels of control of major factors of production exercised by them.

The idea is to establish the extent to which private or collectively owned capital has dominated the economic arena even from pre-colonial Nigeria.

A glance at the structure of pre-colonial economies of communities in Nigeria indicates an economy driven more by individuals as basic economic units, rather than a wholly knitted economy jointly owned by the community or publicly. The situation however varied in conditions in Northern, Western and Eastern Nigeria.

A scrutiny would reveal the existence of some form of community-based and owned structures that carried out specific economic functions intermittently. A seemingly developed market system embodying the essentials of an economy was also discernible.

Ogunremi, (1996) posits that factors of production such as capital, land and labour were effectively organized and utilized in production the process that existed in pre-colonial Nigeria. He also argues those pre-colonial Nigerian entrepreneurs, rulers, chiefs, potentates, war chiefs and other influential persons who had the capacity to mobilize other factors of production.

Nnoli, (1986) identifies the age-grade system that operates in some parts of Igbo land as one of such community based economic systems. Such groups do carry out some economic activities which include the provision and maintenance of infrastructure such as roads and bridges for the community.

Such contributions, most times, do not come with financial reward. They were selfless efforts towards the development of communities.

Members of the age-grade groups do engage in their own economic activities, mostly farming and crafts for their subsistence.

As Ake, (1981), asserts, some form of money such as gold, dinars, copper rods, and cowries were put to limited use as means of exchange.

This suggests, to a large extent, the existence of a significantly developed market system operating side by side with a subsistence economy.

The existence of a sophisticated market system in pre-colonial Nigeria, according to Michael, (2015) was the reason ancient Nok terracotta, Benin bronze casts, Kano cloth weaving and dyeing, Awka blacksmiths and Igbo-Ukwu bronze casts existed famously. For these industries to have flourished, Michael argues, the main factors of production: land, labour, capital and entrepreneurs must have existed in pre-colonial Nigeria.

No wonder then that Nigerian communities and kingdoms, especially those in riverside and coastal areas, as well as those in Northern tips of the country were active participants in trans-Atlantic and trans-Sahara trades

This was the state of affairs in pre-colonial Nigeria before the advent of the colonialists. The first set of Europeans that established contact with Nigerians carried out trading activities that was based on exchange of tropical spices, gun powder and some other goods for slaves.

This was the origin of the cargo mentality. The chiefs and natives looked forward to the arrival of the colonial cargo carrying wines, cigarettes, tobacco gun powder, walking sticks clothes etc.Whenever the ships were sighted, the people went wild with jubilation.

Since then, anybody returning to or visiting Nigeria is always looked upon with the eye of receiving the white man's gift. This, perhaps, is the origin of the 'foreign is better mentality or beggar mentality' among Nigerians.

For centuries, economic relations between Europeans and Africans took this format. The Royal Niger Company, with George Goldie as the chief coordinator emerged as the organized group that oversaw trade between Europeans and Nigerians. The company had the political authority over the then Niger area bestowed on it by the British government.

The Royal Niger Company was formed in 1879, and as Ajayi, (1999) observe, was instrumental to the formation of colonial Nigeria.

The situation changed in 1900 when the British formally took over political administration of Nigeria. The major determinant factor for the direction of the colonial Nigerian economy was the need to ensure continuous flow of raw materials and agricultural produce to the United Kingdom.

And so, the two economic development plans adopted by the British colonialists, the ten-Year Plan of development and welfare for Nigeria, 1946-1956, and the 1955-1960 plan allocated resources to this objective. Helleiner, (1966).

Government therefore concentrated public resources on provision of support infrastructure such as transport and communications, while the private sector was entrusted with the task of establishing and running productive activities.

This situation was reflected in the very first effort towards development planning in Nigeria by the British colonial masters in 1945. After the new Labour government assumed office in Britain at the end of the Second World War, it issued instructions to the colonial administrations, including Nigeria, to prepare formal plans for development.

This was seen by Okigbo, (1993) as obviously informed by the need to ensure guaranteed flow of natural resources. Ravaged by war, Britain urgently needed reconstruction. The colonialists therefore wanted steady flow of the much-needed resources from the colonial territories for this purpose.

This was later modified to government's direct participation in productive activities by the setting up and running of industrial and agricultural enterprises. That was after the colonialists realized that indigenous capitals and businesses were yet to develop the necessary productive capacity for that purpose. Example includes the many marketing boards for the cash crops that several parts of the country were massively producing.

The ten-year plan of development and welfare for Nigeria, a development plan that came up in 1946, according to Ogunjimi, (1997) focused on building a transport and communication system, while little provision was made for industrial development. Also, the plan was selective on its focus on agriculture, with attention on some cash crops, such as cocoa, cotton, groundnut and timber,

That was the reason that led to a dominant public sector in Nigeria. The situation continued deep into Nigeria's independence era. Successive governments operated state-led economies with little contributions by the private sector. No wonder then that the different national development plans drawn up and implemented between 1962 and 1985 were largely dependent on public sector funding.

For instance, in the 1962-1968 Plan, out of the 2.1 billion Naira projected capital expenditure, the public sector was saddled with the responsibility of contributing 1.3 billion Naira. The private sector was expected to pool 780 million Naira. It was a similar situation with the Fourth National Development Plan, 1981-1985. Out of a capital expenditure cost of 82 billion Naira, the public sector was allocated 70.5 billion, while the private sector was to source for 11.7 billion.

The dominance of the state in Nigeria's economy during this period does not pre-suppose that the private sector was dormant. They had a good foothold on the economy.

The many private organizations that existed and were active participants in pre-colonial Nigerian economy continued with expansion in the then newly independent state. They include United African Company, John Holt, Paterson Zochonis, Lever Brothers, Leventis etc.Ajayi,(1999). They were joined by some indigenous companies that operated mostly in transport, retail and marketing end of the economy. One of such was Sir Louis Odumegwu Ojukwu. He was considered the wealthiest person in Nigeria at that time. He was also the country's first recorded Millionaire. He also founded Ojukwu transport, Ojukwu stores and Ojukwu textiles.

He rose to become the first and founding president of the Nigerian Stock Exchange as well as the president of The African Continental Bank.

The policy of import substitution instituted by the Nigerian government after independence also helped to tighten state control of the country's economy. The idea was to make the economy less import dependent by building industries that could manufacture products and plants that were heavily imported. This expanded Nigeria's manufacturing sector as several industries sprang up across the country. Ake, (1996).That was how the likes of ANAMCO, PAN, NITEL, NEPA several steel companies came into existence.

Very huge was government's involvement in the business of the country that between 1973 and 1999, it had invested about 100 Billion US Dollars in 590 public enterprises. Iweala, (2012).

Further government control and dominance of the economy was achieved through the policy of nationalization. A key example was the take-over of British Petroleum and change of its name to African Petroleum by the Nigerian government during the Murtala/Obasanjo military regime.

The indigenization policy of 1971 did not carve out new sphere of influence for the private sector. What rather took place was transfer of private sector ownership from foreign capital to local ones. As Ogbuagu, (1983) asserts, the Nigerian state merely intervened to displace foreign monopoly with local ones. The objective was to set the stage for greater participation by Nigerian nationals in the ownership, management and control of the productive enterprises in the country.

And so, Nigeria's economy in the first few decades after independence was one in which thestate dominated of its ownership of the commanding heights. Over time, state officials saw thisas an opportunity to amass wealth. Subsequently, corruption, inefficiency, nepotism, wastefulness and low morale bedevilled the public service, the main instrument that drives government's business.

This trend continued with progressive negative impact on the structure of the country's economy. High commodity prices prevented a steep manifestation of the negative impact.

The situation however changed drastically in early 1980s. That was when the boom ended abruptly as a deep-seated economic stagnation and crisis set in. Olukoshi, (1993). This crisis rapidly engulfed industries, agriculture, Nigeria's payment position, domestic price level and general living conditions.

The change in the economic fortunes of Nigeria was quite dramatic. An economy that had steadily recorded positive economic growth rate suddenly went into recession. In 1982, Nigeria's GDP contracted by 0.35%. The downward trend continued the following year with a negative GDP growth rate of -5.3%. It did not fare better in 1984 with -5.19%. NCEMA, (2000).

Shift to the Private Sector

It was glaring that the structural shocks that hit the Nigerian economy required realignment. Efforts by the Shagari and Buhari/Idiagbon administrations to use a combination of austerity measures and cost saving schemes to bring the economy back to life yielded limited results.

While the Shagari administration enacted the Economic Stabilization (Temporary Provisions) Act in 1982, whose essence was to reduce government expenditure and curtail imports, the Buhari/Idiagbon regime between 1984 and 1985 introduced more rigorous austerity measures and reverted all imports placed on open licence by the Shagari administration to specific licence. Olukoshi, (1993).

The emergence of the Babangida regime in a coup d'état in 1985 witnessed a radical change in Nigeria's economic management and re-engineering strategy. After the option of a loan from the International Monetary Fund was rejected through a national debate, the regime interpreted it, so it claimed, to mean that the only option was the introduction of Structural Adjustment Strategy, SAP.

The programme was a prescription of the IMF and World Bank for many third world countries that suffered serious balance of payment problems. As the name suggest, it was intended to ensure adjustments in Nigeria's economy.

Its main features included currency devaluation, trade liberalization, freezing the prices of goods and services, financial sector deregulation, privatization and commercialization and public expenditure cuts. Umoren, (2001).

The introduction of SAP in Nigeria was an opportunity for the private sector to make more in-roads into the Nigerian economy. It created a window for ownership of critical and commanding heights of the economy. One of the major pillars of SAP was privatization.

Under this scheme, numerous publicly owned corporations and utilities were either wholly or partially sold to private concerns, thus giving them a foothold and a leverage, they previously lacked.

A law was promulgated to give legal backing to the transfer of national assets to private and foreign businessmen. It came in the form of Privatization and Commercialization Decree No 25 of 1988. After the return of democracy in 1999, the Obasanjo administration modified the decree and enacted it as Privatization Act.

A Technical Committee on Privatization and Commercialization was created to facilitate the privatization process. In the final report of the committee, 36 enterprises were recommended for privatization, as listed in the Decree through the sale of their shares in the Nigeria Stock Exchange, NSE.
Below is the list.

Table 1

List of Public Enterprises scheduled for Privatization as captured in Decree No. 25 of 1998.

NAME OF ENTERPRISE	MODE OF SALE
Flour Mills of Nigeria PLC	PRIVATISATION
African Petroleum PLC	,,
National Oil & Chemical Marketing Co. PLC	,,
United Nigeria Insurance Company	,,
NEM Insurance Co. PLC	,,
Niger Insurance Co. PLC	,,
West African Provincial Insurance Co. PLC	,,
British American Insurance Co. PLC	,,
Crusader Insurance Co. PLC	,,
Guinea Insurance Co. PLC	,,
Law, Union & Rock Insurance Co. PLC	,,
United Nigeria Life Insurance Co. PLC	,,
American International Insurance Co, (Nig) PLC	,,
Prestige Assurance Co. Nig. PLC	,,
Royal Exchange Assurance Nig. PLC	,,
Sun Insurance Nig. PLC	,,
Nigerian Yeast & Alcohol Manufacturing PLC	,,
Ashaka Cement Company PLC	,,
Okomu Oil Palm Co. PLC	,,
Benue Cement Co. PLC	,,
National Salt Co. of Nig. PLC	,,
AyipEku Oil Palm Co. PLC	,,
Unipetrol PLC	,,
Cement Company of Northern Nig. PLC	,,

ABATEX PLC	„
ImpresitBakolori PLC	„
Durbar Hotel PLC	„
FSB International Bank PLC	„
NAL Merchant Bank PLC	„
First Bank of Nigeria PLC	„
International Merchant Bank PLC	„
Union Bank of Nigeria PLC	„
Savannah Bank of Nigeria PLC	„
Afribank Nig. PLC	„
Allied Bank of Nigeria PLC	„
United Bank for Africa PLC	„

Source: Final Report of the Technical Committee on Privatisation & Commercialisation, Volume two

The Technical Committee on Privatization and Commercialization also slated 35 Enterprises, also as listed by the Privatisation Decree No. 25 of 1988 for commercialization. 24 were for partial commercialization, while 11 were for full commercialization.

The Decree defined commercialization as the reorganization of enterprises wholly or partly owned by the federal government in which such commercialized enterprises shall operate as profit-making commercial ventures without subvention from the federal government.

It went ahead to define full commercialization as enterprises that would be expected to operate profitably on commercial basis and be able to raise funds from the capital market without government guarantee. Such enterprises were expected to use private sector procedures in the running of their business. Partial commercialization on the other hand was an Enterprise that was expected to generate enough revenue to cover operational expenditures. The government would consider them for capital grants to finance their capital-intensive projects.

Below is the list of enterprises scheduled for either partial of full commercialization.

Table 2

List of Public Enterprises scheduled for Commercialization as captured in Decree No. 25 of 1998.

NAME OF ENTERPRISE	MODE OF COMMERCIALIZATION
Nigerian Railway Corporation	Partial
Nigerian Airport Authority	,,
Nigerian Electric Power Authority	,,
Nigerian Security Printing & Minting Co. Ltd	,,
National Provident Fund	,,
Nigerian Machines Tools Ltd	,,
Federal Housing Authority	,,
National Iron Ore Mining Co. Ltd	,,
Delta Steel Company Ltd	,,
Ajaokuta Steel Co. Ltd	,,
Rivers Basin Development Authorities	,,
Kainji Lake National Park	,,
Federal Radio Corporation	,,
Nigerian Television Authority	,,
News Agency of Nigeria	,,
Nigerian National Petroleum Corporation	,,
Nigeria Telecommunications Ltd, NITEL	Full
Nigerian Mining Corporation	,,
National Insurance Corporation of Nigeria (NICON)	,,
Nigerian Coal Corporation	,,
Nigerian Reinsurance Corporation	,,
National Properties Ltd	,,
Tafawa Balewa Square Management Committee	,,
Nigerian Ports Authority	,,

Source: Final Report of the Technical Committee on Privatisation & Commercialisation, Volume three.

In another round of the sale of public enterprises, a Privatization Council headed by the vice president was constituted. A total of 111 enterprises were slated for sale with the Bureau of Public Enterprises, BPE, saddled with the responsibility of fast-tracking the process. It served as the secretariat of the National Council on Privatization, NCP and was charged with the overall responsibility of implementing the Council's policies and programmes.

The BPE was established by Decree No. 28 of 1993. The Technical Committee on Privatization and Commercialization submitted its report in 1993 and recommended the establishment of the BPE which should inherit its functions.

The Public Enterprises (Privatization and Commercialization) Decree of 1998 was an upgrade of the earlier Decree.

The NCP is a think tank of the Nigerian government that determines the political, economic and social objectives of privatization and commercialization of Nigeria's public enterprises. It is chaired by the Vice President of the country.

Between the year 2000 and 2014, 143 enterprises were given out wholly or partially to the private sector, according to documents sourced from the BPE.

See full list on Appendix B

A greater chunk of Nigeria's commanding heights was thus handed over to the private sector, in the process giving it a stronger foothold on the Nigerian economy. That perhaps, marked a new turn in terms of public/private sector holding in the Nigerian economy.

Out of the total number that shifted to private ownership and control during this period, 10 of them were given out to core investors. 42 went out by way of core investor sale, while another 10 were liquidated. One enterprise went through the process of guided liquidation.

Thirty-four others changed hands by the mode of concession, with 12 enterprises also through mineral concession.

A further break down indicates that one enterprise went for revalidation of sale, another by the mode of shares sold to institutional investors on the floor of the Nigeria Stock exchange, one by sale to existing shareholders, while nine went by way of shares floatation.

One enterprise was sold off through public offer of shares at the stock exchange, nine through assets sale, and one through willing buyer/willing seller mode. One other enterprise was sold through core investor willing buyer/willing seller initiative, while eight went off by way of private placement. The remaining two were sold off through private placement and debt equity swap.

With this wave of massive privatization, private capital made some breakthrough into some sectors that were hitherto the exclusive preserve of state ownership. A classic example is the electricity sector. The sale of majority equity in the generation and distribution segment of the sector was the biggest privatization effort in the whole world as the proceeds were the biggest haul in any privatization effort globally.

The monopoly enjoyed by the government before the gale of privatizations came to an end. But it threw up a big debate as to whether the privatization scheme achieved its objectives.

Whatever the true situation, it does not remove the fact that most of the firms that benefited from Nigeria's privatization process were special purpose vehicles hurriedly put up for the purposes of taking over previously state-owned utilities.

Most of them were not directly involved in the core business that the enterprises they took over were operating in. A scrutiny of their ownership structure reveals that they were populated by members of the political class who apparently exploited their positions in government and the ruling class to corner for themselves valuable public owned enterprises and utilities in the guise of privatization.

The argument of the proponents of privatization is that the scheme broke government monopoly on critical sectors with its attendant inefficiency.

What privatization succeeded in doing in some instance was to transfer state monopoly to the private sector, thus enriching cronies who paid little or no tax to government.

A critical example is the electricity sector. The generation and distribution companies shifted from major public ownership to private ownership in 2013.It was dubbed the largest privatization transaction in Nigeria and one of the largest in world history. Peterside, (2013) stated that over 400 billion Naira was realized in the transaction that saw 11 distribution companies (DISCOS) and seven generation companies, (GENCOS) transferred to private ownership. The sector was not opened for competition as with the case in the telecommunication sector.

It created an oligopoly, as a few operators took over the monopolistic tendencies of their predecessor company, the Power Holding Company of Nigeria, PHCN. The ideal would have been privatization alongside deregulation. A deregulated power sector would have opened the sector to allow for the participation of several organizations.

States of the federation, private individuals and small-time operators would have joined the generation and distribution of electricity, even off the national grid as a way of creating a more conducive atmosphere for fair competition in the power sector. But the reality is that due to the nature of laws guiding the electricity sector, an unlicensed entity is prohibited from selling electricity to end users.

This may explain why the situation has not changed in the quantity and quality of generation and distribution of electricity more than two years after privatization of the five years sector. The increase in electricity tariff in late 2015 was resisted vehemently by the people who argued that it came without noticeable improvement in supply situation.

While one school of thought agreed that the privatized enterprises are worse off with the attendant impoverishment of the masses, another school is of the view that the state of post privatized enterprises has improved, thereby creating jobs and taking off the financial pressure from public funds.

Abhuere, (2015), argues that privatization in Nigeria excluded the state from the greatest source of strength of development by the divestment of public equity in strategic enterprises. He posits that the situation has sent the state on a long recess, alienating its citizens from it. The resultant effects of non-performance of the privatized companies are loss of jobs and poverty.

The argument of Malo, (2015) typifies the many in support of Nigeria's privatization of key enterprises. In a reaction to assertions of Abhuere, (2015), Malo is of the view that the non-performance of some privatized companies was down to the harsh macro-economic environment occasioned by negative actions and inactions of government.

He also refers to a report in 2008 by DFID and IBTC which indicated that 68.9% of privatized enterprises between 1999 and 2009 recorded appreciable performances.

From Privatisation to Concession (Public Private Partnership, PPP)

The Nigerian bourgeoisie in collaboration with some of their foreign counterparts effected control of major utilities in the country using the guise of privatization. As I argued earlier, being parasitic, they preferred the easy option in the penetration of the economy. Very few of them opted to build industrial and commercial empires from scratch. Like scavengers and hyenas, they preferred to feed fat on the badly managed public utilities which they took over through privatization.

After successfully buying up the utilities, most times in questionable circumstances, and at ridiculously low prize, and having not much to pick on again, their next strategy was to continue the plundering of the Nigerian state by way of concession or PPP. The argument to justify this development has been that government had no place in business.

The sale of firms in the power sector in Nigeria in 2013 left the government with little utilities to operate and manage. The private sector had effectively assumed control of keys sectors such as electricity, oil and gas, mining, telecommunications, vehicle assembly, financial services, etc.

Despite the mass privatization of public utilities, the economy of the country was still far from its desired situation. The much talked about capital inflow, expertise and efficiency associated with private sector led economy were nowhere to be found. Several studies by many public and private institutions noted the huge gap between expectations and deliverables.

The vision 20:20:20 economic development blueprint, a long-term economic development programme put together by the government in partnership with private sector interests stressed the idea of a further transfer of operations undertaken by public institutions to private concerns. It desired a completely private sector led economy.

As Anakwue, (2015) opines, one of the critical policy frameworks that the vision identifies is the expansion of investments in critical infrastructure. It lines out encouragement of private investments as a means of achieving this. Emphasis will be on building on the framework for infrastructure concession where private sector organizations would be allowed to build, maintain, rehabilitate, operate, transfer or own public infrastructure.

The primacy of the private sector in the implementation of the vision was underscored by the huge role it was expected to play. For instance, the first implementation plan of the vision, aggregate investment projections were put at 32 trillion Naira. The federal government is expected to put in 10 trillion naira while the states would contribute nine trillion Naira. The private sector's contribution to this projection is 13 trillion Naira.

As at September 2011, the private sector was only able to invest a mere one percent of the sum it was expected to put into the implementation of the vision.

The plan stated in the Vision20:2020 was first mentioned in another economic development plan, Vision 2010 economic development plan, created during the administration of late General Sani Abacha.

The Vision mandated the government to concentrate on creating an enabling environment that will stimulate private sector saving and investments. It prescribed that the private sector must become the engine of growth of the economy, and this could be achieved through undertaking higher level of investments. It also envisaged that the private sector should support the government in a truly progressive partnership.

The Nigerian government National Integrated Infrastructure Master Plan, a roadmap for building world class infrastructure that would guarantee sustainable economic growth and development in the country was developed and launched in 2014.

It stated that Nigeria would require 3 trillion US Dollars over the next 30 years to achieve an ideal global benchmark of a core infrastructure. That is 70% the country's GDP.

Just as with the Vision 20:2020 economic blueprint, the Infrastructure plan envisaged a public private partnership through concession of public utilities that would provide the much-needed funds for the delivery of infrastructure.

The Obasanjo administration, as part of its reform of the Nigerian economy had anticipated that concession was the future driver of the country's economy. It established the Infrastructure Concession Regulatory Commission (ICRC) in 2005 to cater for private sector participation in the development, financing, construction, operation or maintenance of federal infrastructure or development projects through concession. The commission was also to exercise oversight functions over concessions in Nigeria.

According to the ICRC a PPP concession contract is one that makes the private sector concessionaire responsible for the full delivery of the specified infrastructure services in a specified area, including operation, maintenance, collection, management, and construction and rehabilitation of the system.

Importantly, the private sector is responsible for all capital investments. Although the private sector is responsible for providing the infrastructure asset, such assets are owned by the public sector even during the concession period.

The public sector is responsible for establishing performance standards and ensuring that the concessionaire meets them. The public sector's role shifts from being the service provider to regulating the price and quality of service. The concessionaire collects the tariff directly from the system users.

The tariff is typically established by the concession contract, which also includes provisions on how it may be changed over time. In rare cases, the government may choose to provide financing support to help the concessionaire fund its capital expenditures. The concessionaire is responsible for any capital investments required to build, upgrade, or expand the system, and for financing those investments out of its resources and from the tariffs paid by the system users. The concessionaire is also responsible for working capital.

A concession contract is typically valid for 25–30 years so that the operator has enough time to recover the capital invested and earn an appropriate return over the life of the concession. The public sector may contribute to the capital investment cost if necessary. This can be an investment "subsidy" (i.e. viability gap funding) to achieve commercial viability of the concession.

The National Policy on Public-Private Partnership describes PPP as a government service or private business venture which is funded and operated through a partnership between a government and one or more private sector companies through the PPP route.

It also says the PPP arrangement seeks to allocate the tasks, obligations, and risks among the public and private partners in an optimal way, such that the risks associated, and the costs incurred are minimized and the quality of the infrastructure and services provided are improved.

The distinction between concessions and other forms of PPP is that concessions transfer some or all the demand and revenue risks of the public service to the concessioner, whereas these risks are usually retained by the public sector in other forms of PPP.

For a performance-based PPP contract where the asset requires rehabilitation and maintenance only, such as an existing road, the financing costs will be relatively small and probably provided by the contractor. Where the PPP contract requires the constructions of a significant new asset, however, financing will often be provided by third parties such as banks.

There is a fundamental difference between PPP and privatization. In a privatization, existing assets are transferred to private sector. Legislation determines how services are provided to the public, often with an independent regulator set up to monitor and, in some cases, control prices and prevent market abuse. The regulator may issue licenses that specify service standards and the framework for relations between the concessionaire or private provider. The regulator's functions will sometimes extend to overseeing competition and to ensuring that social welfare objectives are met.

In a PPP, the government retains ultimate responsibility for the public service but will delegate many of the operational tasks to private sector service providers under contract. The contract will determine the service obligations, although a regulator may impose sector-wide requirements, for example, in relation to safety or environmental standards. The contract will also determine how public policy aspects are to be dealt with, particularly if there are to be user charges.

Privatization and PPPs are forms of private sector participation in infrastructure service delivery. However, in PPPs the public sector retains underlying ownership of the asset and accountability for service delivery, while physical asset provision and service delivery are provided by the private sector in line with the PPP contract agreement. Risks and rewards in a PPP are allocated and shared in line with the PPP contract between the public and private sectors.

Privatization refers to the partial or full divestiture of government ownership of an asset. Thereafter asset maintenance and service are determined and provided by the new private owners. No risks and rewards are shared between the public and private sectors in privatization. The new private owners carry risks and rewards conferred by their full or partial ownership of the asset.

There are various forms of PPP arrangements. They are as follows:

Build, Operate, Transfer (BOT)

BOT is a kind of specialized concession in which the private sector or private sector consortium finances and develops a new infrastructure project or a major component according to performance standards set by the public sector.

There are many variations of BOT-type contracts in literature and usage. Under BOTs, the private partner provides the capital required to build the new facility. Importantly, the private operator is said "to now own the assets for a period set by the contract"Sufficient time is therefore allowed for the private sector developer to recover investment costs through user charges. Subject to manipulation, greed and abuse

The public sector may in some cases, agree to purchase a minimum level of output produced by the facility to guarantee the private sector ability to recover its costs during operation. BOTs generally require complicated financing packages to achieve the large financing amounts and long repayment periods required. At the end of the contract, the public sector assumes ownership, but can opt to assume operating responsibility, contract the operations responsibility to the developer, or award a new contract to a new partner.

The distinction between a BOT-type arrangement and a concession, as the term is used here, is that a concession generally involves extensions to and operation of existing systems, whereas a BOT generally involves large "Greenfield" or fresh investments requiring substantial outside finance, for both equity and debt.

Concession

A concession makes the private sector operator (Concessionaire) responsible for the full delivery of services in a specified area, including construction, operation, maintenance, collection, management, and rehabilitation of the system. Importantly, the operator is now responsible for all capital investment.

Although the private sector operator is responsible for providing the assets, such assets may or may not be publicly owned during the Concession period. The public sector is responsible for establishing performance standards and ensuring that the Concessionaire meets them. The public sector's role shifts from being the service provider to regulating the price and quality of service.

The concessionaire collects the tariff directly from the system users. The tariff is typically established by the concession contract, which also includes provisions on how it may be changed over time. In certain cases, the government may choose to provide financing support to help the concessionaire fund its capital expenditures.

The concessionaire is responsible for any capital investments required to build, upgrade, or expand the system, and for financing those investments out of its resources and from the tariffs paid by the system users. The concessionaire is also responsible for arranging the working capital. A concession contract is typically valid for 25-30 years so that the operator has enough time to recover the capital invested and earn an appropriate return over the life of the concession.

The public authority may contribute to the capital investment cost, if necessary. This can be an investment subsidy (Viability Gap Financing) made to achieve commercial viability of the Project. Alternatively, the government can be compensated for its contribution by receiving a commensurate part of the tariff collected.

Lease Contract

Under a lease contract, the private partner is responsible for services in their entirety and undertakes obligations relating to quality and service standards. Except for new and replacement investments, which remain the responsibility of the public authority, the operator provides service at his expense and risk. The duration of a leasing contract is typically five-ten years and may be renewed for up to 20 years. The responsibility for service provision is transferred from the public sector to the private sector and the commercial and financial risks for operation and maintenance are borne entirely by the private sector operator. In particular, the operator is responsible for losses and for unpaid consumers' debts. Leases do not involve any sale of assets to the private sector.

Management Contract

A management contract expands the services to be contracted out to include some or all of the management and operation components of the public service (i.e., utility, hospital, port authority, etc.). Although the ultimate obligation for service provision remains with the public sector, daily management, control and authority are assigned to the private partner or contractor. In most cases, the private partner provides a working capital, but no financing for investment.

The private contractor is paid a predetermined rate for labour and other anticipated operating costs. To provide an incentive for performance improvement, the contractor is paid an additional amount for achieving pre-specified targets. Alternatively, the management contractor can be paid a share of the profits. The public sector retains the obligation for major capital investments, particularly those required to expand or substantially improve the system. The contract can specify the discrete activities to be funded by the private sector. The private partner interacts with the customers, and the public sector is responsible for setting tariffs

Service Contract

Under a service contract, the government (public authority) hires a private company or entity to carry out one or more specified tasks or services for a period, typically one to three years. The public authority remains the primary provider of the infrastructure service and contracts out only portions of its operation to the private partner. The private partner must perform the service at the agreed cost and must typically meet performance standards set by the public sector.

Governments generally use competitive bidding procedures to award service contracts, which tend to work well, given the limited period and narrowly defined nature of these contracts.

Under a service contract, the government pays the private partner a pre-determined fee for the service, which may be based on a one-time fee, unit cost or other basis. Therefore, the contractor's profit increases if it can reduce its operating costs, while meeting the required service standards. One financing option involves a cost-plus-fee formula, according to which costs such as labour are fixed, and the private partner participates in a profit-sharing system. The government is responsible for funding any capital investments required to expand or improve the system.

Agbamuche-Mbu, (2016) also states that various forms of concession models for public private partnerships, PPPs exists. According to her, the most popular among them is the build, operate, transfer, BOT model. Others include build, operate, own, (BOO) model, design, build, operate, (DBO) model, joint ventures, (JV), build, lease, transfer, (BLT), and build, own, operate, remove, BOOR, etc.

Agbamuche-Mbu, (2016) describes PPP as a long-term contract between a private party and a government entity for providing asset or service, in which the private party bears significant risk and management responsibility, and remuneration, is linked to performance.

Under Public Private Partnership, PPPs, the public sector usually determines the services it requires and provides specific benchmarks. The private sector bears the risks of determining the assets that will be required for the project and takes charge of managing and operating the assets.

The private sector bears the financial burden of the project unless the public sector takes equity with a special purpose vehicle, SPV. A Special Purpose Vehicle means the collaboration of several independent firms that come together to register a purpose-specific company, that is, a project-specific consortium.

The companies involved enter into a contractual agreement that specifies their roles and obligations in executing the goals ahead of them. SPV's are also called Single Purpose Vehicles. The public-sector transfers control of the assets to the private sector. It only reverts to the public sector if there is no extension of the concession period.

The Infrastructure Concession Regulatory Commission, the agency saddled with the responsibility of coordinating the concession of projects in Nigeria in December 2016 published a list of 77 projects it hoped to give away.

Under concession, key infrastructure in roads, railways, ports, aviation etc were planned to be transferred to private sector control and management. They are at various stages of development. Only two are at procurement stage, while75 others are at development stage as at 2017. See full list on Appendix C

Outside the list from the concession regulatory commission, the state of two concession agreements between private sector operators and the Nigerian government, perhaps explains in great details the state of, and performance of concession as a means of managing and operating infrastructure in the country.

One case serves as a good example of this: the concession of the Lagos-Ibadan expressway. The road which is the oldest and busiest busy dual carriage highway in Nigeria was transferred to Bi Courtney in form of concession.

The company was supposed to rehabilitate the strategic road, expand it and make it more modern and recoup investment and profit through tolling of the road. Several years after the concession was signed and activated, the firm was unable to carry out any meaningful work on the road.

Usigbe, (2012) reports that the federal government was forced to cancel the concession agreement in the face of non-performance by Bi Courtney.

The same firm also won a concession contract from the Nigerian government to build, operate and transfer a new domestic terminal at the Murtala Mohamed airport in Lagos. Though the terminal is up and running the firm has been having running battle with government over alleged violation of certain clauses in the concession agreement.

Continued and full-scale operation of the concession idea will further enable the comprador bourgeoisie to continue to milk the ordinary people and ensure further collapse of infrastructure and public amenities.

For instance,Wiliams, (2011) reports that the ministry of Aviation had some running battles with Bi Courtney over allegation of exploitation of users of the aviation facilities by way of unilateral and unfair hike in passenger service fees by as much as 150 percent.

1.   The choice of firms for concession contracts is not in any way driven by merit or objective criteria. It is entirely based on patronage. Bi Courtney, the firm that benefited from the two main concession deals in Nigeria hasWale Babalakin, legal adviser to late president Umaru Yar'Adua, as its Chairman.

CHAPTER TWO

Theoretical Perspective

Theories abound in the field of political science. Few, as should be expected, enjoy universal acceptability and applicability. One of such is the Theory. It's very highanalytical and prognostic utility stand it out among others as a tool of analysis. The theory's emphasis on primacy of material conditions in any social relations fits into the rhythm of this work. The importance of the principle of surplus value is very critical to this study as it explains the basis for the exploitation of the masses by the comprador bourgeoisie.

The theory is perhaps, the only one that derived its name from its proponent, Karl Marx. One of the unique features of the theory is that adherents to its principles run into millions and are drawn from outside the field of political science, as well as social science.

These ideas exert a decisive influence on all aspects of human endeavour and have transformed the study of society.

Mukherjee and Ramaswamy, (1999) are of the view that Marxism changed the whole of social sciences and humanities by successfully establishing a link between economics and intellectual life.

Karl Marx, a German political thinker and philosopher, lived in his native country, as well as in England and France during his life time. His theory is based upon the materialist conception of history. Nelson points out that for Marx, any valid historical analysis must begin with the ways in which human beings reproduce themselves.

Jhingon, (2007) refers to it as the materialistic interpretation of history. This, he argues, is an attempt to show that all historical events are the result of a continuous economic struggle between different classes and groups in the society. And with his theory, Marx establishes that poverty and disparities are products of human relations, and not natural occurrences.

From the materialist perspective, Marx analyses the economic mode of production and notes that each generation inherited a mass of productive forces, and a set of social relations which reflected these productive forces.

Together with his bosom friend, Fredrich Engels, Karl Marx developed the concept, otherwise known as historical materialism, where he posits that all historical events are the result of a continuous economic struggle between different classes and groups in the society. The main cause of this struggle is the conflict between the mode of production and relations of production.

The mode of production refers to arrangement of production in a society that determines the entire social, political and religious ways of living. The object of labour, that is, mostly raw materials to which human labour is applied, and the means of labour; the instruments such as tools and equipment that man applies to the raw materials, jointly constitute the mode of production.

The relations of production highlight the class structure of a society, or as Ake, (1981) puts it, social relations of production refer to the relation which people enter during production.

He cites the example of the relations between the peasant and the feudal lord during production. Membership to a class in the society is therefore a function of the above. For Marx, the relations of production are constituted by the division of labour as different productive tasks are related to different people you find classes. You find classes when a small intellectual class separates from the mass of manual labour; such a separation is instigated by the relations of production.

In a capitalist society which Marx did a detailed criticism of, there are the rich and the poor. While the rich owe the means of production, the other only has labour power. The two are referred to as the bourgeoisie and the proletariat.

Relationship between these two classes is one of class struggle. It is typified by the worker or proletariat who sells his labour power to the bourgeoisie who owns the means of production. The product of the interaction is profit. The bourgeoisie appropriates the surplus value to himself. This is after paying the worker for his labour, payments that are less than what his labour produces. That surplus value is supposed to have been shared between the two, but it goes to the bourgeoisie.

How is this surplus value generated? Giddens and Held, (1982) elucidate the process. In common with other commodities, the value of labour power is determined by the amount of labour time necessary for its production.

In the case of labour power; the brain and muscle supplied by the worker, this amount of labour time represents how much the capitalist must pay the worker for services provided. Surplus value is generated by the amount of labour time left over when the employer has recouped the cost of the wages of the worker. In a working day of ten hours, if the cost of paying the worker is recovered after six hours' work, the remaining four hours' production is appropriated by the capitalist as surplus value.

This relation is therefore clearly one of inequality, domination, exploitation and antagonism. It goes on and on, thereby expanding the gap between the haves, and the haves not. It is also replicated in other spheres of societal life: politics, religion, law etc.

It will be pertinent to outline the interdisciplinary nature of the Marxist political economy theory. It takes systematic account of the interactions of the different elements of social life, especially economy, the sub structure and its determinant, the super structure: the political, social and legal systems.

The Marxist political economy theory is also concerned with how the state or its equivalent allocates economic resources within the society.

Goddard et al, (1996) also take Marxist political economy to mean ways in which the social, economic and political aspects of the society interact. It is concerned with how the state and its associated political processes affect the production and distribution of wealth, and how political decisions and interest influence the location of economic activities.

In this process, there is an intensive interaction between major two concepts: state and market.

This interaction is expressed by their two conflicting goals; the market seeks to locate economic activities where they are most productive and profitable, while the state, represented by the dominant class, the bourgeoisie, is propelled by the need to capture and control the processes of economic growth and capital accumulation.

The accumulated capital becomes an exclusive preserve of the dominant class as they are guided by the principles of territoriality, loyalty, and exclusivity. This inequality in the production process is replicated endlessly in all aspects of societal life; in the distribution of income, the distribution of political power, the allocation of status, etc.

Leslie, (1960) provides further insights into how the state and its structures and institutions are employed in the advancement of the interest of the dominant class. He argues that the power generated in the economic sphere, through exploitation, was merely transferred into political power. Political considerations are therefore subordinated to economic ones.

Powers of the state, Leslie posits, were generally made to serve the interest of the bourgeoisie. And as the struggle for economic resources continues in the society, the dominant class tries to enlist the powers of the state in its support.

Van De Berg, (1998) expresses similar views. He asserts that the upper class in every society owns a disproportionate amount of the wealth and contributes a disproportionate number of its members to the controlling institutions and key decision-making groups of the country.

Domhoff, (1979) also argues in the same vein. He describes the ruling class as not merely having a disproportionate influence on the political process, it effectively dominates the process. It imposes its policies and programmes on the lower-class members of the society. He also links the vast advantages major corporate interests enjoy over the rest of the population owing to their control of decision-making processes.

He is also of the view that the owners of these corporations and their surrogates dominate, and are over represented in the executive, legislative, and judiciary branches of the government. This influence he argues, is extended to the ivory towers, media and other critical segments of the society.

The lower class in the society is left at the mercy of the propertied class. They cannot keep up with the competition and struggle for resources.

Miliband, (1969) argues that the competition is not on equal terms. He asserts that big businesses enjoy a massive and decisive advantage in the unequal competition. The propertied class employs its control and influence to thwart any attempt to change the status quo system and ensures that reforms are limited to only those that will not threaten its hold on the resources.

Jiang J,(2007) is of the view that the fundamental approach of Marxist political economy is materialistic dialectics, which applies the laws of unity of opposites, the law of quantitative and qualitative change, and the law of the negation to analyse the objective laws in economic phenomena and the nature and changes of economic process.

He also opines that the five methodologies of Marxist political economy are to explain the changes of social system by the contradictory movement of productive forces and production relations, to analyse individual economic activities in the social economic system formed holistically, to determine the nature of economic system by the ownership of means of production, to explain the political and legal systems and ethical rules in production relations, and to realize the unity of rules and results of social economic development in social practice which help us to generalize the changing economic development.

This theory has the best utilitarian and analytical value for this research. It effectively establishes the link and relations between the two antagonistic classes in the society, it also elucidates the nature of the comprador bourgeoisie in Nigeria, especially its attempts to appropriate the resources of the nation to itself using all within its power: huge wealth base and control of the government and economy.

The Marxist economy theory also effectively explains the use of the prevailing economic regulatory framework in Nigeria to advance, protect and consolidate the interest of the comprador bourgeoisies. The arguments of the scholars we quoted above supports this.

The struggle between the comprador bourgeoisie and the lower class in Nigeria in contemporary times is very glaring. This is despite the clouding of the selfish actions and policies of the upper class in a smokescreen to hide its original objective.

The use of the Marxist political economy for this work will elucidate these issues and make them discernible. It proves that the social contract in Nigeria has failed as it works by entrenching the interest of the elite class. As Marx points out, the state is but the management of the common affairs of the bourgeoisie.

The state in Nigeria, thus, becomes the instrument of the ruling class as defined in terms of the control over the means of production and allocation of value. Therefore, those that hold power in Nigeria want to hold onto it to impoverish the people to determine and define the directions of politics.

Soludo, (2005) also opines that the commanding heights of the Nigerian economy are concentrated in the hands of government. Government then becomes the quickest means of making money. This, he argues has thrown up a rentier state, intensifying politics of sharing rather than production. Garba. J, (1995) had succinctly alluded,

In Nigeria, the manipulation of public policy for private purposes comprises yet another disjunction in our fractured history.

Not every public policy fails, and not every public project or programme is redundant. But, when occasionally that a policy succeeds, it is not often because of government per se, but inspite of it.

The dominant social class in Nigeria will not survive outside government patronage and use of apparatus of the state for primitive accumulation of value. One can therefore understand its desperation to maintain the status quo, as not doing so would amount to economic suicide. The current economic regulatory framework is just one of their means of staying afloat.

Because the Nigerian state cannot create real wealth due to its poor production base, it only serves as a mechanism for the sharing of existing wealth, mainly proceeds from mineral resources. The sharing has been lopsided in favour of the dominant class.

1. The prevailing economic regulatory framework in Nigeria is structured to ensure the protection and advancement of the interest of the elite. Having transferred public enterprises and utilities to their own hands in the guise of privatization, commercialization and concession, they have gone ahead to ensure that the regulatory institutions that would have ensured competition and protection of public.

CHAPTER THREE

Nature of Regulatory Institutions in Nigeria

The privatization of public utilities in Nigeria and the gradual introduction of concession have thrown up the need for the existence of very robust, ethically sound and committed regulatory institutions. The absence of that is capable of eroding national welfare, the welfare of the masses, and fair competition.

Before the era of privatization and concession, when the government dominated most sectors of the economy, the operator ended up also as the regulator as they were most times, the sole operator in the different sectors. Think of the defunct NITEL. It existed without a regulator in the telecommunications industry. The only form of supervision came from the ministry of Communications.

With the intensification of the privatization process during the Obasanjo administration, the need for the creation of regulatory bodies for the telecoms sector arose. And so, the Nigeria Communications Commission, NCC was establishedin 2003 by an act to regulate the telecommunications sector. The Nigeria Electricity Regulatory Commission, NERC was established by the Electricity power sector reform act of 2005 for the purposes of supervising the electricity sector. The Pension Commission was established in 2004 to supervise and regulate the new contributory pension scheme. The National Lottery Commission came in to oversight the lottery business, Department of Petroleum Resources for the downstream sector of the Petroleum industry, Nigerian Civil Aviation Authority, NCAA for the aviation sector, Independent National Electoral Commission for political parties, Medical and Dental Council of Nigeria for the medical profession, Bureau of Public Procurement for public contracts awards, National Insurance Commission for the insurance industry and National Universities Commission for universities in the country.

Other regulatory bodies in Nigeria include National Board for Technical Colleges, Electricity Management Services, Nigeria Nuclear Regulatory Authority, National Bio-Safety Management Agency, National

Environmental standards and Regulatory Enforcement Agency and Nigeria Electricity Management Services, etc.

Some other regulatory bodies that sprang up include the National Broadcasting Commission, NBC and Infrastructure Concession Regulatory Commission, ICRC, as noted above.

Some other regulatory institutions, such as the Security and Exchange Commission were in existence even before the reforms introduced in the Nigerian economy in the 2000's.

Notwithstanding the existence of these regulatory institutions in Nigeria, operators and players in the different sectors of the economy operate with some form of impunity, disregarding and disrespecting the guidelines, rules and directives of their regulators.

This is down to the apparent weaknesses of the regulators, a situation blamed on several factors. Chief among them is the weak legal framework setting up the agencies. Their enabling acts were hurriedly put together, with the government of the day in a rush to push reforms through. Billswith several undefined provisions and regulatory loop holes were rushed to the parliaments for enactments into law.

The Obasanjo administration was in a hurry to reform the country's inefficient and nearly comatose public sector. Credit must however be given to the far-reaching reforms it introduced. But, the pressure to achieve a lot and promptings by Breton Woods institutions led to fast-tracking of the reforms process.

The government in 2001, through the Bureau of Public Enterprise, BPE, set up a steering committee on competition and anti-trust reforms in Nigeria as part of the haste to ensure that the necessary regulatory institutions were put in place against the background of private sector intrusion into the country's economy.

Wilson, (2005) however notes that the mandate and terms of reference of the committee included preparation of draft legislation to eliminate monopolies, remove restrictive conduct and foster competition in all economic sectors and establish a regulatory agency for each sector. This was however not achieved, forcing the government to adopt a half-hazard approach to the building of regulatory institutions in the country.

The problem continued with the lawmakers. The absence of the legislative arm of government during the period of military dictatorships thwarted and stunted its development. It has been struggling to institutionalize the business of law-making since the restoration of democracy in 1999.

The result was a legislature that was most times cajoled by the government of the day into doing a wishy-washy job on the bills without due diligence and necessary scrutiny. The output, just as the initial weak bills that were sent, is also weak and lacking in legal thoroughness that blocks loopholes and ensures smooth enforcement of the provisions of the acts.

When the laws setting up the regulatory institutions were being enacted, the lawmakers were alleged to have been compromised by the executive which wanted to push through the reforms, interest groups which wanted watered down regulators that made them less accountable, and even greed by which legislators were allowed to nominate key staff and management of the newly created institutions.

Inadequate intellectual and knowledge capacity of some individual lawmakers and absence of a robust institutional memory and experience on the part of the then newly established parliament equally affected the process.

Although it is generally accepted that laws are generic and can always be improved upon by amendments, the quick calls for the amendment of some of the acts setting up the regulatory institutions speak volumes of the quality of legislations achieved in the first place.

Let's take the case of the Infrastructure Concession Regulatory Commission. It was established by an act enacted in 2005. It seeks to provide for private sector participation in the development, financing, construction, operation or maintenance of federal infrastructure or development projects through concession and contractual arrangements.

As Anakwue, (2015) observes, the law does not confer on the commission the powers to stop or challenge any concession agreement undertaken by any Ministry, Department or Agency that it considers detrimental to national interest.

Nigeria's national interest will be compromised where government agencies, which most times lack requisite personnel and expertise to negotiate complex PPP projects with multinational organizations with unlimited resources, are left solely to do so.

The implication is that the MDA's were given far reaching powers to negotiate and consummate concession agreements on behalf of the federal government. The ICRC can only watch helplessly if infractions are noticed in the process of PPP's.

Agbamuche-Mbu, (2016) also highlights weaknesses in the ICRC act. She is of the view that it failed to provide a detailed set of regulations for the PPP project approval process and the procedure for the grant of a concession under the act.

She also notes that the powers granted to the commission are limited to keeping the signed concession agreements and monitoring their implementation.

She further advocates for the expansion of its powers to include overseeing the evaluation process for PPP projects and enforcement powers.

Another factor responsible for the weakness of regulatory institutions in Nigeria is their subordination to politics. They are tied to the aprons of the executive arm of government in terms of formulation of policies and programmes, as well as guidelines in day to day operations.

A scrutiny of the acts establishing the key regulatory institutions in Nigeria indicates that the president of the country does directly, or through cabinet ministers exercise suzerainty over them.

In the Nigeria Communications Commissions act of 2003 that established the Nigeria communications commission, NCC, part 1 section 23 states the functions of the minister of communications to include,

(a) the formulation, determination and monitoring of the general policy for the communications sector in Nigeria with a view to ensuring amongst others, the utilization of the sector as a platform for the economic and social development of Nigeria;

(b) the negotiation and execution of international communications treaties and agreements, on behalf of Nigeria, between sovereign countries and international organizations and bodies; and

25-(1) subject to the subsection (2) of this section, the minister shall, in writing, from time to time notify the commission or and express his views on the general policy direction of the federal government in respect of the communications sector.

The same goes for the electricity power sector reform Act of 2005. The act established the Nigeria Electricity Regulatory Commission; the regulators of the electricity industry.

In section 33, the act empowers the minister of communications to issue general policy directions to the commission concerning electricity, including directions on overall system planning and coordination, which the commission shall take into consideration in discharging its functions.

This, no doubt, negates the real essence of regulation in any economy. A regulator is supposed to be neutral, objective and should transcend the sector it is supervising. Where political control is brought in as we explained above, it introduces shocks and disequilibrium.

The regulators confidence and independence take a huge beating. Players with political or any other affiliation with political heads will enjoy unfair advantage, thus creating an uneven playing field.

The case of the multi billion dollars fine imposed on MTN, one of the telecommunications service providers in Nigeria by the regulators of the sector, National Communications Commission, NCC became controversial once the minister of communications Adebayo Shittu, Chief of staff to president Mohammadu Buhari, Abba Kyari, and even the president himself stepped into the fray.

Negotiations on possible reduction of the fine and modalities of its payment were taken away from the NCC and carried out within the AsoRock Presidential Villa, Abuja.

The action was no doubt legal as the NCC act gives the minister such latitude. It however came with some drawbacks.

Regulating a sector in Nigeria's economy will serve the nation's interest better if an appreciable level of independence is guaranteed the regulator. A former Secretary to the Government of the Federation told me anonymously that independence of the regulatory agencies would not be a reality as it is a threat to handing out patronages by government officials.

Before the advent of the regulatory agencies, when government dominated businesses in Nigeria, award of licenses, contract deals, and allocation of resources were at the discretion of government officials. The regulatory agencies have nearly taken away this power from political office holders. Since government has remained a means for primitive accumulation of wealth in the country, those in government would stop at nothing in ensuring that the neutrality and objectivity of regulatory agencies are undermined. Their selfish financial interests always override wider national interests.

It is not all regulatory agencies in Nigeria that lack independence, at least on paper. Some of them that enjoy, in quote, some form of independence conspicuously stand out. The first is the Fiscal Responsibility Commission, FRC.

The commission serves as regulators to ministries, agencies and parastatals, MDA's, in that it ensures and enforces prudent management of the nation's resources, long term macro-economic stability of the national economy, greater accountability and transparency in fiscal operations within a medium-term fiscal policy framework and promotion of Nigeria's economic objectives.

It was clearly stated in section 1, subsection (2) that the commission shall be independent in performance of its functions. Though appointed by the president and confirmed by the senate, its board enjoys full independence in carrying out its prescribed roles.

With this independence, the commission can, upon realization that a public officer or institution violates the provision of fiscal responsibility act, forward a copy of its investigation to the Attorney General of the federation for possible prosecution.

Another case of a regulatory body in Nigeria with an even greater degree of independence and autonomy in operations is the Central Bank of Nigeria (CBN).

The independence enjoyed by the bankers' bank was because of the amendment of its act in 2007. Its monetary policy committee is the highest decision-making body, especially with formulation of monetary and credit policies for the Nigerian economy.

The bank has over the years demonstrated the autonomy conferred on it by its enabling act. It has exhibited little or no influence from the president and federal cabinet members on issues of fixing of monetary policy rates.

The Pension Commission is yet another regulatory body that is immune from presidential interference. The institution regulates, supervises and manages the administration of contributory pension system in Nigeria.

Perhaps, due to the widespread economic and social impact which its operations have on the Nigerian society, the operational responsibility of the management is directed by the board. The pension commission came after the enactment of the 2004 Pension Reform Act. The promoters of act were guided by the need to reform the inefficient pension system ran by government that was at a state of near collapse.

The need to limit political interference prompted autonomy in its administration and management of the pension system. This is without prejudice to the fact that annual report of its activities is sent to the president and the public accounts committee of the national assembly.

Another pitfall faced by regulatory institutions in Nigeria is lack of quality personnel. Appointments into the boards of the institutions are clearly the prerogative. Some of their enabling acts do prescribe the nature of qualifications needed, but this is grossly inadequate to guarantee that the best hands are picked.

Political considerations in their appointments rob the country of the much-needed quality manpower to drive regulatory activities in critical sectors of the nation's economy. Party men and women exert all manner of pressure on the president to concede appointments to their cronies, thereby compromising standards and competence. Some CEO's of regulatory agencies in Nigeria are card-carrying members of political parties, mostly ruling parties. Some others that were not initially politicians begin to eye and do contest for political offices at some point in their tenure or completion of it.

Regulatory activities should be knowledge driven. Clear understanding of the nuances, complexities, intricacies and nitty-gritty of the sector is not only imperative, but mandatory for efficient operation of the sector.

Every regulated industry is dynamic. It is constantly transformational. So, even experienced and competent regulators may not be enough to transcend the sector and serve as a leviathan. A continuous update of knowledge base and better understanding of international best practices will help to keep the dialectical operating environment in check.

These are compromised once extraneous, political and sometimes primordial considerations pre-dominate merit in the choice of leadership of regulatory institutions.

This malaise continues deep down the entire structure of regulatory bodies in Nigeria. There have been several cases of secret employments of cronies of management staff and political leaders. There have also been numerous cases of sale and purchase of employment letters in these institutions. With all these put into consideration, it would only be foolhardy to expect an efficient, world class regulatory institutions in Nigeria.

Staffers of regulatory institutions find themselves in an inferior position against the players in their sector. They are supposed to transcend the sector they are regulating, but they are only entangled and enmeshed in the mix.

Perhaps, the biggest stumbling block and pitfall of regulatory institutions in Nigeria is the high level of influence and controls operators in the different regulated sectors wield over their supposed regulators. This is a situation where the organizations that are supposed to be regulated end up regulating the regulator.

Through various means, the decisions, policies, programmes and dictates of the regulatory institutions are tailor made by some powerful and influential operators. These influences also come by way of inability and refusal of the regulators to wield the big stick and mete out punitive sanctions on operators that infringe on, and violate rules, regulations and codes. It could also come by way of dishing out privileged information to an operator by a regulator, which most times gives the operator anedge over others.

Suffice to say that this practice is not peculiar to Nigeria. Even developed and strong economies such as the United States of America also fall prey to this. Several scholars have researched on the subject to the extent that it earned George Stigler a Noble prize.

The conclusion of Stigler is that regulated agencies captured by the industries they regulate are worse than no regulation at all, since capture gives the industry the power of government.

Due to the relative newness of most regulatory institutions as highlighted earlier, the board membership and even staffers of regulatory institutions are drawn mostly from operators. This inevitably creates an uneven level playing field.

The requirement of full disclosure, complete cutting of ties with former employer before staff of a regulator is employed, and the oath taking to be fair to all are made to mitigate possible conflict of interest. This has not fully addressed the problem.

The initial chairman of the board of the Infrastructure Concession Regulatory Commission, Ernest Shonekan was an active participant in Nigeria's private sector. The same also goes for many of the Governors of the central bank. Notable among them are the current governor, Godwin Emefiele who managed Zenith Bank, and Joseph Sanusi who also served as Managing director of First Bank. Sanusi Lamido Sanusi, who was also a CEO of First Bank before being appointed Governor of the apex Bank,

Much of the allegation of bias in favour of parent company and background of the chief executives rarely get to public domain as the fear of reprisal actions prevents victims from crying out loud.

Privileged information in terms of policies and programmes does sometimes get to certain operators who take full advantage by way of anticipatory moves. A scrutiny of the profit pattern of these companies when their former executives head regulatory institutions, which burgeons during their time in office, further gives rise to suspicions of insider information.

Most of the staffers of regulatory institutions in Nigeria are cross-over's from operators in the same industry. They are mostly those that are nearing retirement, those seeking a more rigorous and demanding jobs, and those that have been edged out in power plays in their original employments.

Top management staff of regulatory institutions receives "kind gestures" from operators in their industry. It can be by way of sponsored foreign trips to attend conferences, seminars and workshops. Some other times, monetary gifts do exchange hands, while certain privileges are often also traded.

There are weighty allegations that top-brass of regulators of the telecommunications industry are given free airtimes by operators. The same allegation was also raised against regulators of the broadcast industry who are accused of enjoying free subscriptions from operators of multi pay TV operators.

The remuneration of employees of regulatory institutions is sometimes lower in value compared with those of operators in their sector. This breeds inferiority complex and serves as a disincentive for greater efficiency. Some of the institutions such as the Fiscal Responsibility Commission's salary scale is of the civil service standards. The Salaries, Incomes and Wages Commission approved a special salary scale for the Fiscal commission, but this was not implemented.

As Sanjour, (2012) notes the knowledge by staffers of regulatory institutions of the influence big corporations wield both within government and outside inadvertently cajole them into submitting to their interests.

Regulatory agency employees soon learn that drafting and implementing rules for big corporations means making enemies of powerful and influential people. They learn to be "team players", an ethic that permeates the entire agency without ever being transmitted through written or oral instructions. People who like to get things done, who need to see concrete results for their efforts don't last long within regulatory institutions.

The fraudulent collusion of the operator with regulators erodes national interests. The masses are usually the worse for it. This is exemplified with developments in Nigeria's capital market between 2005 and 2012. This was the period of economic "boom" when several companies went public for the first time, raising billions of capitals from the market.

It was also the same period that existing players in the market also raised fresh capital, mostly financial institutions struggling to meet up with the new capital base requirements prescribed then by the Central Bank of Nigeria.

The Security and Exchange Commission, SEC, is the regulatory body for Nigeria's capital market.

From every indication, the commission was not at its best, in partnership with players and issuing houses, to uphold and protect the interest of the investing public.

The prices at which shares of the companies were fixed by the issuing houses were approved by the Security and Exchange Commission. There were suspicions that the prices were overvalued.

It is the responsibility of the regulatory commission to carry out adequate due diligence in approving the price at which shares will be sold to the public.

No wonder then that the true values were achieved months after the conclusion of the initial public offer, rights issue and share offering.

It did not take long before the bubble burst. The fake high prices fell like a pack of cards before the investing public knew what was happening.

The average all share index of the Nigerian Stock Exchange in 2007 stood at 57,990 points, according to an annual report of the Nigeria stock exchange for that same year. Three years later, there was a noticeable and drastic change in the value of shares in the stock exchange as it fell steep down to 24,770 in 2010. This represents a loss of more than half of its value. The loss in share value contrasts sharply with the GDP performance of the country during the period. In 2007, Nigeria's GDP was 226 billion US dollars. It went up to 330 billion in 2008, but stood at 297 billion US dollars in 2009, before settling at 369 billion in 2010. So, how does one explain that at a time Nigeria's GDP growth rate was improving, signifying an economic boom, the share value of its stock exchange was on a free fall.

Let's look at the situation in Ghana during the same period. In 2007, the Ghana stock exchange all share index was 6,595.63 points. Three years later in 2010 it stood at 7,360.21 points. This represents an increase. How do we then explain the differences in fortunes of shares in these two West African countries, other than a weak regulation of the Nigerian stock market, leading to connivance by stake holders to short-change the investing public.

The period between 2006 and 2009 marked the era of massive activities in Nigerian stock exchange. That was the period of recapitalization of banks. It was also the same period that several private companies went to the stock market to raise funds in initial public offers. Other blue-chip companies also took advantage of the rush for shares and weak regulations in the stock market to raise extra funds. It was more like a fake bubble led boom as many Nigerians started trading activities in the stock market.

If the regulatory institution in the Nigerian stock market, the Securities and Exchange Commission, was on top of its game, we should not have recorded this steep loss in share value. From all indications, the share prices of the companies were simply unrealistic.

The argument that the global financial meltdown experienced during the same period played a big role in the massive loss of value of stocks in Nigeria may not be cogent enough. Yes, the meltdown did take its toll on other stocks around the world, but how do you explain how these other stocks experienced boom when the global economy picked up, and Nigerian stocks remained static.

Unlike Nigeria, Ghana, a fellow West African country, made concerted efforts to develop its regulatory system. Its government in 1991 formed the private sector advisory group, PSAG, tasked with the responsibility of examining existing laws and regulatory procedures which impeded private sector investment and development. It was to advise the government on relevant revisions of obstructive laws and to develop a set of specific recommendations for legal reforms. Asem et al, (2013).

The group set to work, and its recommendations were implemented by the government. Ackahet al. (2010). This no doubt ensured that Ghana was better prepared than Nigeria in terms of the establishment of an efficient regulatory system in the light of private sector entrance into its economy.

Reforming Nigeria's Regulatory Institutions

Regulatory environment in any economy is constantly dynamic. Even if Nigeria's regulatory institutions operate at world's best standards, there is every need for continuous reforms to align them with changing times. Sociologists always remind us that change is constant, and I cannot agree less.

The existence of the world is tied to continuous and unimpeded changes and evolutions. If the world comes to a standstill, it will come to extinction. It is continuous change that gives life to the earth.

The earth itself makes two movements on its axis that sustain its existence. The first is rotation. When the earth rotates around the sun in about 24 hours, we get night and day. Imagine what will happen if the earth stops this rotation. One part of the hemisphere will be constantly exposed to the sun, while the other will be exposed to extreme cold and darkness.

The second movement of the earth is revolution. It revolves around the sun in about one year, giving us the different seasons. If this revolution is halted, we will then have continuous rainfall or harmattan without changes. The consequence is better imagined.

The smallest particle in the earth is an atom. This, just like the earth itself, is dynamic. Its constituent parts, the electron, proton and neutron are in a continuous and dialectical interaction. This is what gives life to the atom.

So, for Nigeria's regulatory institutions to function effectively and efficiently, they must be continually reformed. The economic objectives of the country will be far from being realized if the regulatory institutions fail to live up to expectations. This is even more imperative as the country's economy is substantially private sector driven.

Wilson, (2005) posits that the quality of a country's legal regimes and regulatory institutions has a direct bearing on its economic performance.

The first step towards reforming Nigeria's regulatory institutions is to carry out a comprehensive review of the acts setting them up. There is every opportunity to correct the anomalies and pitfalls contained therein.

The first step is to look at the powers and influence wielded over the CEO's by the president. It is true that the executive powers in Nigeria, according to section 5 (a) of the 1999 Nigerian constitution is wielded by the president who is also the commander in chief of its armed forces.

Section 171 (d) of the same constitution also empowers the president to appoint head of extra-ministerial departments of the government of the federation, howsoever designated.

Besides the constitutional provisions, the different acts setting up the regulatory agencies give the president the power to appoint their CEO's and members of the boards. They are therefore subordinated to influence and control of the president. Most of the acts establishing the regulatory Agencies give the minister overseeing them or the president powers to advice on specific and general operational directions.

The CBN option is the way out. The act establishing the apex bank was amended in 2007, based on the promptings of former president Olusegun Obasanjo to confer autonomy on it.

The bank has since then enjoyed full autonomy in handling and managing Nigeria's monetary policies. It has maintained this tradition even in the face of attempts by key government officials to influence its activities.

At the height of Nigeria's economic recession in 2016/2017, former finance minister, Kemi Adeosun (2016) was quoted to have asked the CBN to lower interest rates to push in more funds into the economy. She believed the more liquid the economy was, the higher its chances of getting out of recession.

As Dada (2016) reported, the suggestion was rebuffed by the CBN which maintained that it needed to tighten liquidity as a means of checking high inflation, then at over 18 percent.

Some lawyers will however argue that granting such autonomy to regulatory agencies may violate the Nigerian constitution that vests executive powers on the president. Section 5 clearly states that the executive powers of the Nigerian constitution shall be vested in the president.

But, sub section (a) of the same section also boldly states that executive powers vested in the president may be subjected to laws made by the national assembly.

In sub section (b), the constitution also recognizes that executive powers in Nigeria shall extend to the execution and maintenance of the constitution, all laws made by the national assembly and to all matters with respect to which the national assembly has, for the time being, power to make laws.

These provisions in the constitution legitimize the amendment effected in the CBN act in 2007. The act establishing key regulatory institutions in Nigeria should equally be amended to grant them such autonomy.

Further, as a means of conferring some level of independence and autonomy on regulatory institutions in Nigeria, there is a need to guaranteethe tenure of the CEO's and board members.

Again, I refer to the CBN act that stipulates that the governor can be removed from office on the recommendation of the president of the country and two-thirds approval of the senate. The consent of a clear majority of the senate will no doubt raise the confidence level of the institutions and further extricate them from political manipulations and control.

But, the successful operation of this depends to a large extent on the ability of the senate, and indeed other institutions and structures of the society to insist on the observance of the rule of the law. A powerful and dictatorial president will always find the means of emasculating the senate, media and the civil society when he breaches some of the relevant constitutional provisions.

Two cases are good illustrations. The first is the use of presidential fiat to discontinue a plan by the Central bank of Nigeria under Chukwuma Soludo to redenominate the Naira.

The apex bank had planned to redenominated Nigeria's currency, Naira, as was the case with Ghana, as a means of fighting inflation. After it went public with the plans, the then President Umaru Yar'Adua over-ruled the bank insisting that it must stop.

In an interview with the Financial Times of London, Yar'Adua, (2008) claimed the central bank went beyond its authority in going ahead with the plan. To him, it was a clear violation of the law establishing the CBN.

I had earlier established that the Central bank enjoys autonomy and independence on issues of monetary policies. Redenomination of a country's currency falls squarely within the precincts of monetary policy.

Another illustration of the erosion of powers of the Central bank is the suspension and replacement of its former governor Sanusi Lamido. The governor had in a letter that was leaked to the public informed President Jonathan of billions of Dollars the Nigeria National Petroleum Corporation, NNPC, Nigeria's state-owned oil company failed to pay into the country's treasury.

The president reacted with the announcement of the suspension of Sanusi from office. As reported by Vanguard newspaper, Jonathan based his action on a report by the Financial Reporting Council of Nigeria which indicted Sanusi of financial recklessness and misconduct.

The action of Jonathan was in clear violation of the 2017 CBN act as amended. The act requires the senate to approve presidential request for the removal of its governor before it could take effect. President Jonathan was not guided by the law in suspending and removing Sanusi from office.

What the two illustrations above signify is that at its present level of development, Nigeria needs more than laws to ensure the operation of its society based entirely on the rule of the law. The compliance of political office holders with the laws, and more importantly, the ability of other structures and institutions of government to serve as checks and balance each other are equally important.

No doubt, the first step towards achieving a just and orderly society is to put the necessary laws in place. At a later stage in the life of the country, greater adherence to laid down rules, regulations and laws may be achieved. But, for now, there is the need to amend the laws setting up the key regulatory institutions to ensure greater security of tenure with the requirement of senate approval of presidential advice for suspension or sack of CEO's and board members.

As I pointed out earlier, except for the amended CBN act, the Fiscal Responsibility Act, the Pension Reforms Act and the act establishing the Security and Exchange Commission, SEC, the president exercises operational control over the regulatory agencies. The president also sets broad guidelines for the operations of the institutions.

This has remained the source of their inefficiency as sentiments determine their actions. The boldness needed to effectively regulate the different sectors of the economy is absent, as moving against the interest of players in the sector that are sympathetic to government in power, may be interpreted to mean disloyalty.

Furthermore, the knowledge that the presidency may override decisions taken by regulatory institutions is another big hindrance. This leads to inefficiency, loss of confidence and lack of decisiveness on the part of regulators.

The case of a fine imposed on a tele-communications Company, MTN by the regulators of Nigeria's telecoms sector, the Nigerian

Communications Commission, NCC is a classic example of presidency's open interference in the activities of a regulatory institution.

The company was fined 1.04 trillion Naira for ignoring the use of unregistered sim cards. That was after several warnings to disconnect the lines. But, as Okonji, (2016) reported, the fine was reduced to 330 billion Naira after the Nigeria presidency intervened in the dispute between the regulator and the operator.

This was a clear signal to operators in Nigeria's different economic sectors that the regulatory institution can easily be by-passed on matters concerning their sector.

Udo, (2016) asserts that the action of the Nigerian Presidency was a dangerous precedent. He wondered why the NCC was not involved in the negotiations to reduce the fine. The Attorney General of the Federation was at the head of government's negotiation team. He also cautioned that Nigeria must avoid pandering to sentiments other than national interests.

Presidential interference in the activities of regulatory institutions is not restricted to Nigeria. The issue is also of similar concern in the United States, a country that practices same type of a presidential federalist government.

Worsnop, (1969) spotlights how American presidents have tried to influence policy decisions in the country's key regulatory institutions. According to him, every president of the United States, from Woodrow Wilson, has tried in one way or another to influence the activities of the big seven regulatory agencies, and have succeeded in doing so.

The big seven regulatory commissions in the US are the Interstate Commerce Commission. The commission's jurisdiction covers railroads and related carriers, the Federal Trade Commission that deals with preventing practices leading to trade monopoly or restraint of trade and the Federal Power Commission that grants licenses to private power projects.

Others are the Federal Communications Commission that regulates telephone, security and exchange commission that regulates security and the stock market, National Labour Relations board that adjudicates on unfair labour practices, and the Civil Aeronautics Board that licences domestic air carriers.

Cushman, (1941) also noted how President Hoover made public comments indicating how he thought the Interstate Commerce

Commission ought to exercise certain of its powers, and the commission somewhat reluctantly yielded.

Percival, (2011) also reasons likewise. He asserts that most regulatory statutes in the US specify that agency heads, rather than the president, shall make regulatory decisions. But he still wonders why yet, after more than four decades, every president has established some programme to require pre-decision review and clearance of Agency regulatory decisions, usually conducted by the office of Management and Budget.

He also explained how President Obama on January 18, 2011 joined his seven predecessors in expressly endorsing regulatory review when he signed executive order 13,563.3.

The order claims that it requires that federal agencies ensure that regulations protect safety, health and environment while promoting economic growth. It also ordered a government-wide review of the rules already in the books to remove what is considered outdated regulation that considered stifled job creation and competitive economy.

It is quite clear that presidents do go against the laws of their country in the exercise of their powers. Illustrations from Nigeria and the United States lend credence to this assertion. Despite provisions in the laws establishing regulatory bodies empowering the management and board as final authority on policy issues and operations, presidents do violate the laws.

It appears that there is confusion between the powers of the regulatory institutions and those of the president.

Calabresi, and Yoo, (2008) also analysed this constitutional issue. They proposed that even if the president has unfettered removal authority of regulators management and board, the removal does not imply the power to control decision making entrusted by law to agency heads.

In other words, the law must be sacrosanct. If it guarantees autonomy to regulatory institutions, it must remain so. Any president that finds it inconveniencing should simply seek amendments to regain control.

Presidents in presidential systems of government do rely on the fact that executive powers are conferred on them to issue executive orders and proclamations that tend to erode the independence and autonomy of regulatory agencies and institutions.

According to a publication by Civic and Education Literacy, executive orders are not specifically mentioned in the constitution of the United States, but have been used by every president since George Washington-more often in times of war or during national disasters, when government policy needed to work more quickly than the traditional process.

The Supreme Court has, however, sometimes, stepped in to rein back presidential use of executive powers. Executive orders are directives handed down from a president or a governor without the involvement of the legislature or judiciary branches of government. It can be given to agencies of government.

In Nigeria, executive orders are also sometimes issued. On Friday May 19, 2017, Acting President Yemi Osinbajo issued three executive orders. According to a Proshare Intelligent Investing publication, among the three orders is one on timely submission of annual Budgetary estimates by all statutory and non-statutory agencies, including companies owned by the federal government.

The order demands that all federal government agencies shall, before the end of July every year, cause to be prepared and submitted to the minister of finance and the minister of budget and planning their annual budget estimates, which shall be derived from the estimates of revenue and expenditure as projected in their three-year schedule.

The order also notes that heads of agencies and chief executive officers of government owned companies shall take personal responsibility for any failure to comply with this order.

This is a clear usurpation of the powers and functions of the Fiscal Responsibility Commission. The act establishing the commission explicitly gave it the mandate to compel ministries, departments and agencies to do exactly what the executive order is craving to achieve.

As I stated earlier, the commission serves as regulators to ministries, agencies and parastatals, MDA's, in that it ensures and enforces prudent management of the nation's resources, long term macro-economic stability of the national economy, greater accountability and transparency in fiscal operations within a medium-term fiscal policy framework and promotion of Nigeria's economic objectives.

It was clearly stated in section 1, subsection (2) that the commission shall be independent in performance of its functions. Though appointed by the president and confirmed by the senate, its board enjoys full independence in carrying out its prescribed roles.

With this independence, the commission can, upon realization that a public officer or institution violates the provision of fiscal responsibility act, forward a copy of its investigation to the Attorney General of the federation for possible prosecution.

The Fiscal Responsibility Act stipulates timeline for ministries, departments and agencies on the submission of their annual budgets. This is the same message that the acting president's executive order conveys.

Is it that the presidency is not aware of the provisions in the Fiscal Responsibility Act? Or is it that it acknowledges the failure of the Fiscal Responsibility Commission, the body responsible for the implementation of the Fiscal Responsibility act? Or perhaps, the executive order is meant to reinforce and complement the functions and roles of the fiscal responsibility commission?

This, no doubt is just another violation of the independence of a statutorily independent regulatory institution in Nigeria. Is it the failure of the regulatory institutions in living up to their responsibilities that provides the opportunity for the president to invade and violate their independence? Or is it a calculated and concerted efforts to undermine their operations for pecuniary reasons?

The five-year tenure of the board of the fiscal responsibility commission with JubrinYelwa as chairman expired in 2013. The board provides guidelines for the operation of the commission besides being its highest decision-making organ. Up till May 2017, no new board had been put in place, thus nearly paralyzing its operations. The commission had remained a spectator as ministries, departments and agencies freely violate the provisions of the fiscal responsibility act.

The MDA's and government owned companies are supposed to remit their operating surplus to government treasury. Section 22, sub section 1 of the fiscal responsibility act demands that 80% of operating surplus of the agencies, or four-fifths should be paid into the consolidated revenue fund, while-one fifth or 20% should be retained as operational costs.

This directive has been continually ignored. The Fiscal Responsibility Commission has been weak in enforcement. There is a widely-held belief that the refusal of government to reconstitute the board of the commission since 2013 and the perceived lack of cooperation and support from the government are part of a plot to render it ineffective.

An efficient, functional and powerful Fiscal Responsibility Commission would to a large extent, stop the diversion of government funds by revenue generating agencies and companies. This has regrettably remained a conduit pipe for slush funds.

CHAPTER FOUR

Regulatory Institutions as Fourth Arm of Government

It has become not only imperative, but also very urgent to reform regulatory institutions especially in a country such as Nigeria, where policies such as indigenization, privatization, commercialization and concession have turned the economy from being dominated by government ownership to one under the control of the private sector.

These developments that spanned through several decades came without the necessary institutions to regulate the private sector players and ensure the promotion and protection of national and public interests.

Nigeria wittingly and unwittingly brought in the private sector interest which is monopolistic and strictly profit oriented. It's the place of the regulators to serve as a bulwark against what could become the rampaging private sector interest. Unfortunately, successive governments were not quick in entrenching regulatory institutions same way they were in handing over the economy to the private sector.

With the greater part of the Nigerian economy under the control and influence of the private sector, there is need for the government to retain a measure of control by way of its regulatory institutions. But my earlier arguments have shown how executive interferences have weakened the regulatory institutions and undermined their activities.

There are however arguments that governments do not completely withdraw from participation in their countries' economies even in the face of privatization, deregulation and concession.

Vogel, (1996) is of the view that what is experienced in a deregulated economy is re-regulation. This implies that deregulation does not entirely presuppose that government has detached itself from direct participation in the economy. Rather, it throws up a situation where the economy is regulated the more with the establishment and expansion of regulatory institutions and their operations. As government withdraws from direct participation in the economy, it equally assumes greater roles with the activities of regulatory institutions under its purview.

Mckenzie and Lee, (1991) also raise a similar argument. They see deregulation as merely government relinquishing its regulatory powers to new government institutions. Since the regulatory institutions are still part of government, how then can the argument that government has withdrawn from business stand?

Regulation in an economy driven by the private sector should be protected from undue and petty influences. I have identified the sources of these influences to include the private sector, ruling political party and the presidency.

One method through which this could be one is to create a mechanism that will allow the legislature and the judiciary, and the private sector players have shared control, supervision and oversight of the regulatory institutions in a system of checks and balances, alongside the executive arm of government.

What this means is that all the arms of government will exercise some form of control and supervision of regulatory institutions without any of them having a dominant and preponderant role.

This is made more pertinent considering that regulatory agencies apart from carrying out normal executive responsibilities, do exercise quasi and legislative/judiciary functions. During their operations, some of the agencies make what is regarded as administrative laws. They also impose punishments on operators who violate some of the laws.

When the Nigerian Broadcasting Commission establishes a code for broadcasters and broadcast stations in the country, it is simply making some form of laws. And when it goes ahead to impose fines or suspension of license on broadcasters and broadcast stations, it is inadvertently passing some form of judicial pronouncements.

The body of laws, codes, regulations and rules guiding the broadcast industry in Nigeria are contained in what the Nigeria Broadcasting Commission refers to as Nigeria Broadcasting Code. In the fifth edition published in 2012, the 197-page document details what it refers to as minimum standard for broadcasting in Nigeria.

In the 2004 act that established the commission, section 2 (1) (a) empowers it to determine and apply sanctions, including revocation of licences of defaulting stations that are in violation of the code.

The sheer volume of the rules and regulations contained in the code indicate that the broadcast commission churns out laws without inputs from the National Assembly. In other words, it does not need national assembly input for making laws guiding the sector. There are nearly three hundred of the regulations and rules seen as do's and dont's in the broadcast code.

The National Assembly has not made up to five laws for the broadcast industry in Nigeria. It has unwittingly provided the leeway for the regulator to churn out these laws governing the industry.

This is replicated in most regulatory institutions in Nigeria. They have drawn up hundreds of laws guiding their different sectors.

Wornop, (1969) describes regulatory agencies as the fourth arm of government. He argues that regulatory agencies should be designated as an arm of government as they probably account in sheer volume of legislation and administration done by the American government.

This argument, no doubt, is not misplaced. It has become increasingly clear that regulatory institutions are playing, and still have more crucial roles to play in the Nigerian economy. The idea of designating them as the fourth arm of government, at least informally is to equip them with the necessary legal and institutional framework for greater effectiveness.

Just with the traditional three arms of government, the assumed fourth arm must enjoy some form of autonomy where necessary, and check and balance the functions and powers of the other arms, while also being subjected to the same treatment by the other arms.

There are existing statutory provisions in Nigeria's laws that give the traditional arms of government shared control and influence over regulatory institutions.

For most of them, appointment of their board is a shared responsibility between the executive and the legislature. The power to appoint rests with the president, but it needs the approval of the senate. The president can also relieve the board members of their appointment, but in few cases, such as with the CBN, this requires the consent of the senate.

As I highlighted earlier, the president is still empowered by law to intervene in the operations of the institutions by way of providing general guidelines on broad objectives. The Infrastructure Concession Regulatory Commission Act, 2005 in part vii, section 33 states that the president may give to the Commission such directives of a general nature or relating generally to matters of policy with regards to the exercise of its functions under this Act as he may consider necessary, and it shall be the duty of the Commission to comply with the directive or cause them to be complied with.

What this means is that the president, through his ministers can exercise regulatory function and roles. For instance, the president can order award of licenses, waivers and special treatment for preferred players in different sectors of the economy. Being politicians, there are no safeguards that such actions will not be laced by political considerations. Some may argue that a president may be guided by national interest in such actions, but can it be guaranteed? The question is, how can a level playing field be provided for the different sectors of the economy to thrive? The issue of national interest is subjective and could undermine the constitution.

The problem of Nigeria's economy will persist till a time the country either removes political interferences or at least, moderate them.

The influence of the legislature over the institutions extends to the fact that they appropriate funds for them by way of approving their budgets. Furthermore, the legislature retains additional influence by its powers of oversight and probe of their dealings.

The judiciary also checks and balances the operations of the regulatory institutions by way of review of their actions. Operators can challenge the legality of regulatory actions by seeking judicial interpretations. This is rarely done in Nigeria as the operators believe challenging regulatory decisions in court may harm future relations.

This, no doubt is a setback to efficient operations of the country's regulatory industry. The case of MTN, one of Nigeria's telecommunications company comes to mind. It rushed to court to challenge the decision of the regulators of the telecoms industry in the country, the Nigeria Communications Commission in imposing huge fine on it for failure to disconnect unregistered lines. After some "behind the scene moves" the company quietly withdrew the case from court.

Balance of Interests

One way of strengthening regulatory institutionstions assume the place of the fourth arm of government in the country is by giving operators greater influence and control. A quarter of members of the board of every institution should be nominated by players and operators in the sector.

For instance, in the banking sector, the operators have a common platform known as Bankers' committee under the Central Bank of Nigeria, where issues affecting their sector are dealt with. It is a body of

Chief Executives of banks in the country. It has become an influential body within the banking sector in Nigeria. The body, just like similar ones in other sectors of the economy should be given the responsibility of nominating a quarter of board members of the Central Bank of Nigeria, the regulators of the banking industry in Nigeria, and other regulatory institution in the country.

Operators in an economy, as I earlier asserted, wield tremendous influence over their regulators. The best means therefore of reforming the regulatory institutions is to formalize this influence and control. The operators should have a formal presence and voice within the boards of the regulatory institutions. Allowing an operator or a few operators to continue to wield this influence will lead to monopoly, oligopoly and an uneven playing field.

Operators in the different sectors of the Nigerian economy are critical stakeholders that must be given a formal role to play in the economy. This will no doubt, ensure greater transparency, participation and competitiveness in the operations of regulatory agencies. Their inclusion will check, to a very large extent, the undue influence and control exerted on the regulatory institutions by members of the executive and legislature.

Who can protect the economy more than those whose entire lives are devoted to it? The operators of the economy possess the greatest stake in it, and so if there is any group that will go the extra mile it is those that stand to lose the greatest in the case of any eventuality.

Greater inclusiveness in a country's political economy will raise its level of stability, transparency and competitiveness. With the inclusion of operators in the management of regulatory institutions, all tiers of government and key interest groups would be accommodated in the decision-making process for every sector of the economy. The fusion of the varied interests would serve as a counter-balance and checks on the excesses of other stakeholders.

This inclusion is already underway, although at informal level. The opinion of stake holders is always sought by regulators when critical decisions such as review of codes and guidelines are being carried out. So, why not formalize it?

Critics may raise fears of conflict of interest as reason why the inclusion of operators in the board of regulatory agencies may not be feasible. This argument maybe overlooked if one considers that they are only a quarter of the entire membership of the board. To prevent a situation where they may tactfully take major decisions of the board, the quorum of the boards must be determined by stratified structural basis. This means that quorum during meetings must be based on compartmentalization. That is, a specified number of representations from sub-categories of representation must be achieved, before decisions can be taken. In this way, their influence is counter-balanced at the altar of national or public interest.

Organization of modern democratic societies is arranged in such a way that different interest groups are given stakes. It is also structured in such a way that these interests serve as checks and balance on each other.

The three arms of government modelsare designed along this line. Other groups locate their interest directly or find ways of aligning to protect and promote their selfish interests. It is this interaction, which is dynamic and contradictory in nature that gives life to the society and its stability.

There are talks and moves towards opening the spaces within the politics and economy of every society, as a way of ensuring inclusiveness and by implications, stability in societies. There is every need to create more room and space for the private sector within the Nigerian political economy. There is no better way to do this than guaranteeing them a quarter of the positions in the boards of regulatory institutions in the country. They have over the years, due to the important roles in the economy, become the unofficial fourth arm of government.

This will create more dynamism in the complex web of pursuit of, as well as promotion and protection of interests in the wider Nigerian society, a move that would advance stability of the country.

The inclusion of the private sector or operators' interest within the board of regulatory agencies is key to saving the institutions from the grip and manipulations of politicians.

The promulgators of the public procurement act 2007 incorporated this idea. They included key interest groups outside political appointees into the supposed highest public procurement approval body, the National Procurement Council.

Part 1 of the act stipulates that membership of the council must comprise of minister of finance as chairman. Members include the attorney-general of the federation and minister of justice, secretary to the government of the federation, economic adviser to the president and head of civil service of the federation.

It made provision for membership from outside government, mostly from different interest groups in the nation's economy. Six of them are to serve as part-time members representing Nigerian Institute of purchasing and supply Management, Nigeria Bar Association, National Association of Chambers of Industry, Mines and Agriculture, Nigeria Society of Engineers, Civil Society and the Media.

It is on the same line of thinking that the Fiscal Responsibility Act, 2007 was enacted. The act established the Fiscal Responsibility to oversight ministries, departments and agencies in terms of observance of transparency and prudence in their operations as outlined in the act.

The board of the commission comprises of a chairman to be appointed by the president and confirmed by the senate, and a member representing the private sector, civil society, organized labour and a representative of the ministry of finance.

Is it because of the inclusion of "outside" interest, that is those not appointed directly from the president's area of influence, that the two boards have not been constituted, thereby rendering them ineffective and in a state of comatose? I wonder.

The Procurement Council has not been constituted since the enactment of the Procurement Act in 2007. The federal executive council has continued to usurp the powers and functions of the council by constituting itself as the highest contract awarding body in Nigeria. Ordinarily, the federal executive council's primary responsibility is approving policies and programmes of the executive arm of government.

Is it that the lure of protecting, promoting and advancing pecuniary interest has motivated successive governments since 2007 to continue along this line of illegality? These interests include ensuring that choice and plum procurement contracts go to favoured firms, with utmost disregard to competition, openness and probity.

It is argued these same interests that manifest in government's choice of membership of boards of regulatory institutions. Members, it is believed, are mostly picked to further these interests by ensuring that decisions, regulations, guidelines, codes and rules are tailored to suit specific interests.

The fear in some quarters is that allowing a seemingly independent body to handle the task of approving public procurements will not guarantee continued protection of selfish interests.

It is also due to this consideration that the Federal Government has refused up till July 2017 to reconstitute the board of the Fiscal Responsibility Commission, FRC since the tenure of the last board ended in 2013.

This situation has rendered the commission ineffective and placed it in a position that it cannot enforce fiscal discipline in government's operations. Government officials misapply their administrative and financial powers and go unpunished and unchecked due to the incapacitation of the agency that has the responsibility of whipping them back to line.

Simply put, the government, it appears, has demonstrated uneasiness and intolerance to the idea of relinquishing part of its control of public procurement and enthroning fiscal discipline in its operations.

To ensure an efficient regulatory system in Nigeria, steps must be taken towards moderating the control and influence wielded by government, by incorporating the interest of operators and other key interest groups in the boards and management of regulatory institutions. Successive governments in Nigeria, it is said, have rarely represented public interests and there are fears that it has come to a point where they can no longer be trusted.

A classic example of a regulatory institution in Nigeria that creates room for operator's greater influence and control is the Medical Laboratory Science Council of Nigeria. It has the responsibility regulate the practice of medical laboratory science in Nigeria. This involves the registration and licensing of medical diagnostic centres in the country. The 2013 act provides for a governing board that will oversee the activities of the institution.

It comprises of 19 members. 12 of them are to be selected from among medical science practitioners in the country. The umbrella body of medical science laboratory scientists, known as association of Medical Scientists of Nigeria is to nominate the 12 members of the board to the minister of science and technology, who in turn is mandated to forward the names to the president of the country for formal appointment.

Note that it is compulsory for the minister and president to carry out this responsibility without alteration of nominated persons. It is this board that is under the strict control of medical laboratory scientists that appoints a registrar for the council. The registrar is the chief executive officer of the council.

This effectively places practitioners and operators in the medical laboratory science sub-sector of the larger health sector in a controlling position on the regulation of the industry.

The situation here is far more than my recommendation that a quarter of the board of regulatory institutions be reserved for operators. I spoke to some management staff of the Medical Laboratory Science Council of Nigeria and they made me to understand that the preponderance of the operators on the board has created a near excellent atmosphere for smooth and quick decisions on issues of regulation. This presents an interesting scenario.

Unfortunately, the same lukewarm response government had shown towards the constitution of the boards of regulatory agencies whose enabling acts moderate its control, is also obtainable with the Medical Laboratory Science Council of Nigeria. Is it a mere coincidence as the board of the council is yet to be reconstituted since 2015?

It is the responsibility of the organized private sector to lead the campaign to actualize the restructuring of the board of regulatory institutions to create room for operators. Existing private sector pressure groups such as the Manufacturers Association of Nigeria, MAN, National Association of Chambers of Commerce, Mines and Agriculture, NACCIMA and the many private sector pressure groups in Nigeria should begin a sensitization and lobby campaign to actualize this.

Private sector participation in the management of the Nigerian economy received a big boost during the Goodluck Jonathan administration. The Economic Management team, an elite team of cabinet members and key private sector players, was saddled with the responsibility of formulating economic policies and programmes for the government.

As Okonjo-Iweala, (2018) listed, the 28-member team is comprised of the president as chairman and the Vice President as deputy chairman. The governors of Anambra state, Peter Obi and that of Adamawa state, Murtala Nyarko were also members. Other members of the team were the ministers of finance, petroleum, agriculture, health, national planning, power, transport, trade and investment, works and the chief economic adviser to the president. Others were the presidential adviser on monitoring and Evaluation, Chairman of the Federal Inland Revenue Service, Executive Chairman of Federal Inland Revenue Service, FIRS and Director General of Bureau of Public Enterprises, BPE, Director

General of the Budget Office, Chief of Staff to the President, Comptroller General of the Customs,Director General, Debt Management Office, Director General, Securities and Exchange Commission and the Director General of the Bureau of Public Procurement.

President Jonathan expanded the Economic Management Team to include, for the first time, key members of Nigeria's private sector. They were Aliko Dangote founder of the Dangote group, AtedoPeterside, Chairman of Stanbic IBTC, Tony Elumelu,Chairman of HEIRS Holdings, Jim Ovia,Chairman of Zenith BankPLC,andDr WasilatTitiola ShittuBusinesswoman

Many could not comprehend the rationale behind the inclusion of members of the private sector in the management of the Nigerian economy. Finance Minister and Coordinating Minister for theEconomy, Okonjo-Iweala, (2018), was one of those that did not initially like the idea. After initial hesitation, she saw that the idea to include some private sector players in the Economic Management Team of Nigeria might help the private sector understand the government's need for reforms and persuade them to participate as partners in the reform process.

No doubt, President Jonathan had reasons for carrying out the action. The Jonathan move is completely in sync with our recommendation that operators in every sector of the Nigerian economy be involved in its regulation. The private sector is becoming a greater partner in the development of the Nigerian economy, and its input in the regulation of the different sectors is a sine quo non for steady and inclusive economic development.

Former president Jonathan confirmed this assertion in an interview I had with him on the issue. He said apart from getting key private sector players into his economic team, he also appointed the president of the Nigerian Economic Society his honorary adviser on economy. He believed involving the private sector in economic policies and programmes of the country was very necessary to get their inputs, being the real operators of the economy. Jonathan acknowledged the quality inputs of the private sector members of his Economic Management Team pointing out that at different times, their observations led to alterations of policies, critical points that would have been missed if they were not part of the economic management team.

He said his decision to include them into the team was inspired by the action of former President Olusegun Obasanjo who consulted key private sector players unofficially before taking major decisions on the economy. Jonathan said he went further by including them officially into his economic team.

He however pointed out that their involvement in the economy stopped at advisory and consultative role, as another economic team, the Economic Management Implementation Team had the responsibility of actualizing the decisions of the Economic Management Team, by following up with the implementations.

The Economic Management Implementation Team was chaired by the finance minister and had as members all the Ministers and Directors General in the main Economic Management Team.

Safeguards for Operators Influence in Regulatory System

As I mentioned earlier, bringing in outside interests into Nigeria's economic regulatory system may have its drawbacks. But, the institution of very strong anti-trust laws will check possible over-riding operators influence within regulatory agencies.

Antitrust and competition laws, as Hawke and Middleton (2011) agree, are intended to promote competition and benefit consumers. They are based on the premise that free and open competition promote lower prices and improve the quality and selection of goods and services.

They are also referred to as statutes developed by governments to protect consumers from predatory business practices by ensuring fair competition exists in an open market economy.

Dempsey, (2013) notes that Competition and Antitrust laws prohibit collusion between competitors that restrain, in such areas as price-fixing. He also posits that they prohibit monopolization through mergers, and through anticompetitive means, such as predation or abuse of a dominant position.

Presently, Nigeria still operates without anti-trust laws. Attempts were made in the past to codify and enact anti-trust or competition laws, but the efforts were not very successful or enough to create the desired impact.

There is no legislation or set of regulations that is dedicated solely to anti-trust or competition issues in Nigeria. But, some parts of existing acts have tried to partially provide some form of legal instrument to carry out the function.

Part II, VI and VII, sections 26, 80-82 of the Electric Power Sector Reform Act, 2005, has statutory provisions which seek to provide guidelines regarding consumer service and protection, licence performance, with competition and market provisions.

The Nigerian Electricity Regulatory Commission is expressly required to, on a continuous basis, monitor the Nigerian Electricity market for the potentials that exist to drive additional competition and tariff Regulations in the best interest of the market

A similar situation also exits in the aviation industry, section 30 (4) (i) of the Civil Aviation Act, 2016 authorises the Nigerian Civil Aviation Authority to investigate any case or cases of unfair or deceptive trade practices or methods of competition, including the prices of airline tickets

In the capital market, the Investment and Securities Act, 2007 has provisions which require the Securities and Exchange Commission to prohibit market rigging and manipulations, insider rigging and all other forms of unfair fraudulent trade practices in the Nigerian Stock Market. Oserogho and Associates, (2015)

The first attempt at drafting a holistic law to regulate competition in Nigeria was made by the Bureau of Public Enterprises between 2002 and 2003. Different versions of the draft law have been circulating in the National Assembly. But, the latest version, Federal Competition and Consumer Protection Bill was introduced in the parliament in August 2015. Banwo and Ighodalo, (2016). It has stalled in the National Assembly.

Efforts must be made to fast-track its passage. An effective anti-trust legislation will introduce order and fairness in a private sector led economy.This is even more pertinent considering the prominent role the private sector plays in the Nigerian economy.

As I established earlier, the Nigerian economy, over the last few decades has witnessed a pre-eminence of the private sector over the public sector. This should have been accompanied by a proportionate establishment and development of an efficient regulatory and anti-trust framework for necessary balance of interests, influence, power and control over the economy in public interest.

It smacks of a dangerous neglect for Nigeria's economy that is private sector driven to be operating without strong anti-trust laws and system of regulation. An anti-trust commission should have been put in place even before the implementation of privatization and concession.

Such a commission is necessary to guarantee fair competition and protection of public interest. This fact is elementary even for students of economics and political economy. But, the suspicion that the elite in government used the guise of privatization and concession to corner public enterprises may explain why no drastic action has been taken in this regard.

The new owners of public enterprises would prefer the existing situation: public monopoly transformed to private ones. Any move that will break the monopoly or introduce institutional checks would be resisted and frustrated as the status quo is more beneficial to them than the one that promotes both the public and private interest.

For how long shall we be oscillating in the quagmire? That is the question many people are asking. Clearly, time will tell.

CHAPTER FIVE

Ensuring a Productive Private Sector

I have established how the private sector in Nigeria has been encouraged to achieve a dominant control of the country's economy by being in the driver's seat. I have also proposed how it could be involved in the decision-making process (economic regulatory system) within the economy.

It is however glaring that the nature and character of the private sector in Nigeria is such that it cannot play the role expected of it in a developing economy. That is, become the driver of the economy.The private sector in Nigeria is disarticulated, subservient, and lacking in the rudiments to propel the development of the Nigerian economy.

Despite the inroads made by the private sector in the country's economy, the anticipated impact is still not felt. What obtains is a quasi-private sector that is still in incubation. It is therefore still in the process of development.

According to a ranking of countries of the world on bank credit to the private sector as a percentage of GDP for 2015 by the Globaleconomy.com, a publication of the World Bank, Nigeria performed very poorly. It came a distant 146 out of the 164 countries that were ranked with a mere 14.94 percent. This is a dismal figure compared to Mauritius, the highest ranked African country that posted 102.77 percent.

The bulk of bank credit in Nigeria goes to the government, indicating that the private sector is yet to take effective control of the country's economy, despite schemes by successive governments to put it on the front foot. The financial institutions prefer to advance credits to public institutions through the purchase of more lucrative treasury bills and bonds. Financial institutions in the country rank among the best in Africa. They make the biggest gains and profit in the Nigerian stock exchange, yet, the productive sector in the nation's economy has remained in the doldrums.

For instance, in the first 9 months of 2017, according to Ugwu, (2017) the banking sub-sector emerged the most performing stocks with a gain of 894 Billion Naira. This represents 61.99 percent during the period under review. This was mainly due to sustainable positive sentiment on the banking sector by investors following the impressive half year financial performance.

The performance of the credit exposure of financial institutions to the private sector illustrates its structural imbalance and weak foundations in the country's economy. Bad debts and non-performing loans keep increasing. This may be part of the reasons the financial institutions are shying their doors for enterprises in need of credit,

Abioye, (2017) reports that non-performing loans in banks in Nigeria rose from 1.678 trillion in June 2016 to 2.084 trillion in December of the same year representing an increase from 11.7 percent to 14 percent. Many banks in Nigeria have failed, or are he edge of failure due to their very high and unhealthy non-performing loans.

The huge non-performing loan advanced to the private sector has forced government to consider the shutdown of The National Economic Reconstruction Fund, NERFUND. The fund was established to advance credit to Nigeria's private sector as part of measures to boost the country's economy. Just as non-performing loans has been on the increase with private and commercial financial institutions in the country, the same trend is also prevalent with government owned private sector credit finance scheme.

Muhammed, (2017) reports NERFUND accumulated a 17.5 billion Naira non-performing loans, government commenced plans to wind it up. The fund had advanced loans to finance about 1,143 projects in the small and medium enterprises sector between 2010 and 2013 but ran into problems as most of the loans were performing very poorly.

Something is wrong with business environment in Nigeria to the extent that small, medium and huge businesses struggle to keep afloat. The financial institutions are thus scared of advancing credits to the private sector.

Government has tried to address the lack of finances for the private sector by its interventions in some critical sectors. Several institutions have been established as interventionist agencies to bridge the funding gap created by the refusal of the financial institutions to channels funds to the private sector. They include the Bank of Industry, BOI, National Economic Reconstruction Fund, NERFUND, and Small and Medium Enterprises Development Agency, SMEDAN.

The Central Bank of Nigeria has floated numerous programmes to do exactly what the financial institutions are supposed to do but failed to carry out. There are special funds for textile revitalization and the Anchor Borrowers' programme for small holder farmers.Yahaya, (2017) reports that about 200,000 farmers have benefitted from the 43.9 billion scheme in two years.

The undeveloped nature of Nigeria's private sector is also reflected in its tax to GDP ratio. Adeosun, (2017) noted that at 6 percent, it was one of the lowest in the world. Two factors may be considered here as reason for this low level. It is either the government failed to expand its tax base or that profitability of the private sector was dismally low. Itcould, however, be a combination of the two reasons.

Simply put, Nigeria's poor tax return is an indicator of the performance of its private sector. Governments around the world rely on taxes collected from individuals and firms engaging in productive activity, but Nigeria is largely dependent on revenue stream from sale of crude oil.

Many scholars have therefore concluded that Nigeria operates a rentier economy.

Bello, (2017) describes a rentier state as one that relies on substantial external rent. He is of the view that in a rentier state, the creation of wealth is centred on a small fraction of the society, while the rest of the society is engaged mainly in the distribution and utilization of the wealth created.

Beblawi and Luciani, (1987) argue that getting access to the rent circuit is a greater preoccupation than attaining production efficiency. They also posit that reward-income or wealth is not related to work and risk bearing, rather to chance or situation. The rentier state is oriented away from the conventional role of providing public goods that have been extracted from the people through taxation; it is a provider of favours.

Dlakwa, (2006) explains that a rentier state is one that lives from externally generated revenue or rent from its resources, mostly by external clients rather than the surplus production of its population.

The private sector in Nigeria has been caught up with the rent mentality as the operations of some of them are product of and tailored along the same line with the Nigerian state. They feast on the same rent, taking advantage of every opportunity to get its "fair share" of the rent collected by government from the sale of crude oil. It reflects the

Nigerian state in nature and character. This does not becloud the fact that there are some private sector players that are shining examples and have adopted international best practices in their operations.

Other major reasons why the private sector in Nigeria appears hamstrung are the harsh and strangulating business environment, dilapidated business support infrastructure and uneven environment, external oriented consumption pattern of the citizens, as well as the system of discrimination that regulates management of government-businesses relationship.

Let me begin with the very last factor. The system of procuring licenses, approvals, contracts, registrations, certifications and allocations for businesses in Nigeria is, most times based on discriminatory practices and riddled with corruption. This makes it difficult for most businesses to thrive, not to speak of survival, or profit.

For instance, the operation of a limited liability company in the country demands its incorporation by a federal government controlled Corporate Affairs Commission. This process takes weeks to conclude as red tapes and corruption are constraints.

The business, after registration may demand issuance of a license before commencement of operations in a chosen field. For instance, a company wishing to go into mining must wait for a license from the president of the federal republic through the minister of mining. The issuance of this type of license may take years, depending on the company's political affiliation, status of its owners, and willingness to offer bribes to government officials.

If the organization wishes to apply for land to build its business offices, it must go through the Governor of the state in which it has its operations or the minister of the Federal Capital Territory if it were to be in the nation's capital, Abuja. The allocation of plots in Nigeria has never been based on any objective criteria, but a system of corruption and discrimination. The extant laws guiding it confer lots of discretionary powers on the governors and the president through the FCT Minister. This has been continuously subjected to abuses.

The discriminatory and corrupt practices continue with approval of building plan before an organization that is a beneficiary of a land allocation can put up a structure in it. It takes years for such an approval to be processed, but only a few months if the organization succumbs to requests for bribes.

The list of processes that businesses go through in search of approvals, licenses, allocations and certifications that are muddled in corruption and discrimination goes on. These strenuous and cumbersome processes have negative effects on private businesses in Nigeria. It either makes operational cost too high for them to cope with or throws up businesses that lack managerial and technical competence, such that the businesses do not stand the test of time.

The poor state of the business environment in Nigeria is reflected in ranking of the ease of doing business in countries of the world carried out by the World Bank in 2016.

Nigeria was ranked 169th out of a ranking of 189 countries, with a score of 44.6 percent. The ease of doing business compares economies with one another, the distance to frontier score benchmarks economies with respect to regulatory best practice, showing the absolute distance to the best performance on each doing business indicator.

This type of scenario is replicated in most sectors of the economy. These hindrances strangulate businesses in the country. I earlier advocated the inclusion of the organized private sector interest in regulatory institutions in Nigeria. Most times, it is the institutions that award licenses, certificates, approvals, procurements and allocations. Inclusion of the organized private sector would moderate their excesses, reduce discrimination and increase objectivity.

Efforts must also be made to activate, the operations of the different institutions and structure of the society that serve as checks on the activities of government agencies dispensing services to the private sector and individual business operators. This includes the media and civil society. They have sometimes been too quiet when some Agencies go over the board in their dealings with the public.

Another reason for the poor performance of the private sector in Nigeria is the low demand for goods and services produced in the country because of the external oriented consumption pattern of the citizens. There is a clear preference for foreign goods, and this rubs off negatively on the operations of businesses, especially productive ones in the country.

There is no doubt that the bulk of Nigerians have the ethos to consume. This insatiable urge has a strong preference for foreign made goods. It's more like as a status symbol to be seen patronizing and consuming goods procured from outside the shores of the country. This cuts across all social strata and age groups.

The resultant effect is that local companies have huge stocks of unsold stocks lying waste in warehouses. Due to shrinking demands for local goods, these local manufacturing firms have failed to take advantage of economies of scale to expand operations and cut down on cost of production.

Nigeria boasts of some vehicle assembly plants that have shown promises of metamorphosing into full manufacturing outfits if proper polices are put in place, and patronage sustained, but the country still imports hundreds of thousands annually.

A newspaper report in Vanguard newspaper of June 24, 2013 quotes the director general of National Automotive Council, Aminu Jalal as saying that 200,000 new and used vehicles were imported into Nigeria annually, with about 600 billion naira expended in the process. Think of the impact this amount would make in the local automotive industry if used in the purchase of their products.

New wealth made by citizens, most times through dubious means is squandered on medical tourism and mostly in the consummation of foreign made goods and services. These include designer clothing, wines and champagnes, luxury cars and private jets, foreign holidays etc.

This preference for foreign made goods is more noticeable in government circles where tax payers' moniesare channelled into procurement of foreign products to satisfy the high taste of public officials. There have been campaigns by successive governments for patronage of locally made goods, but it has been more of rhetoric without specific measures being outlined to ensure its success.

The 8th National assembly has been working on an amendment of the Procurement Act to give priority to locally made goods in the execution of government contracts, but action has not been fast enough in this regard. Government can resort to the use of laws and strict policies to compel public institutions to patronize goods manufactured in the country.

The local content act is however a master piece towards creating a local resource base and technology in the oil industry. It also aims to increase indigenous participation in the oil and gas industry by prescribing minimum thresholds for the use of local services and materials and to promote transfer of technology and skill to Nigerian staff and labour in the industry. Legislations such as these are needed to promote and protect our local technology base.

I said earlier that the prevailing culture in Nigeria is ethos to consume. The ethos to produce is not prevalent. Most people would rather spend savings on luxury goods and consumables than invest in a business enterprise or production venture. The spirit of entrepreneurship is not as dominant as it should. This may explain why businesses fail to survive beyond generations.

I had also earlier outlined how the bulk of government's businesses were transferred to the private sector by way of privatization, indigenization and concession. I also tried to explain the dubious manner the enterprises were transferred to the new owners. This is the key problem of the private sector.

Those that took over public enterprises did not emerge through competitive, objective and rational process. Merit was sacrificed on the altar of parochial sentiments.These enterprises ended up in the hands of those that lacked the requisite technical, administrative and managerial competence to run them.

A scrutiny of the owners and board members of privatized enterprises in Nigeria reveals that they are comprised of mostly ruling party stalwarts, former top military officials, and relatives and proxies of serving top government officials.

The sale of distribution companies under the reform of the electricity sector saw the emergence of companies that claimed to possess the requisite technical and financial muscle to manage and turn them around.

A few years after running the DISCOS, it became glaring that the new owners are far from being what they claimed to be. The reality has dawned on the government. Ujah, (2017) reports that the federal government has commenced negotiations with operators of the Electricity Distribution Companies with a view to cede some of their shares to accommodate new investors who would bring in more funds to increase their service delivery.

During privatization of the power sector, the government sold 60% equity to the companies that bought over the DISCOs, while retaining 40%. After realizing that these companies lack the competence to run them, the government is now on the lookout for the "real investors".

The plan is for the government and the operators of the DISCOS to cede some of their equity to the real investors that the companies should have gone to in the first place. This was captured by the minister of state for budget and national planning, Mrs Zainab Mohammed in her statement at the 23[rd]Nigeria economic summit in Abuja on October 12, 2017.

> The power sector has been privatized and every Nigerian knows that the privatization has not worked. Things we sought to achieve in the power sector have not happened. And now, we have come to the point where investors in the power sector must come together and decide to cede some of their holdings to enable new investors with expertise come in to enable us to grow the power sector at the pace we want. It involves negotiating with existing owners and government.

The situation in the power sector signposts the status of most privatized companies in Nigeria. These are the supposed major plank of the economy that moved from public control to private ownership. The intention was for the new owners to run the enterprises at the optimum, thereby making the private sector the engine of growth of the economy.

Attempts to also concession critical public enterprises such as the AjaokutaSteel Company recorded huge failure. For years, the Nigerian government has been battlingGlobal Infrastructure Holding Limited, the company it gave out the huge steel complex to an Indian firm over its ownership. Operations at the complex have remained nearly comatose. The country recently established the Infrastructure Concession Regulatory Commission. This means that more and more public utilities would be given out by way of concession in the years to come. No doubt, the same practice of favouring only friends and associates in the choice of winners of concession bids would continue.

What should be done to reverse this trend? Simple! Centralize the approving authority for concession deals in the country. Based on the act establishing the Concession commission, ministries, departments and agencies can unilaterally see through concession deals. The Regulatory Commission is not even empowered to vet the deals or certify that due process was followed in the choice of the concessionaire, or that public interest was protected in the entire process.

The decentralization I am refereeing to is the amendment of the Infrastructure Concession Regulatory Actto empower the Regulatory Commission and the Public Accounts Committees of the National Assembly to approve of any concession deal before it comes into effect.

The choice of the Public Petitions Committees was arrived at because they were headed by the opposition.

Operationalization of Regulatory Institutions in Nigeria

The next chapter will list and describe the functions of all regulatory institutions at the federal level in Nigeria, but this chapter will outline the operational mechanism or modus operandi of regulatory institutions in the country and will attempt to establish the nature and levels of relationship with and between the Presidency and the Cabinet.

Every regulatory agency in Nigeria is established by law. It could be through a decree or act of parliament. These laws prescribe in detail the objectives, mandates, functions and responsibilities of these regulatory agencies.

It also establishes the management structure, composition of the board, the staff structure, and reporting lines to the presidency through the overseeing minister in some occasions.

The board sits at the top of the organization chart. One of reasons why some regulatory boards have not performed optimally is the absence of their boards. Due to some political considerations and hurdles, successive presidents have wittingly and unwittingly been unable to constitute some boards. These boards remain the highest policy making body for regulatory institutions. In most instances, the president makes appointments into membership of the boards, and in some few occasions, nominations to the boards, usually ratified by the president are done by some interest groups or professional associations

In the absence of the boards, the supervising minister assumes full responsibility. But this has not always been very effective as some of the enabling laws of some regulatory institutions are strict on the approving authority of the board for most actions. This renders the management of the agencies incapacitated in taking sensitive actions and decisions.

The management of the regulatory agencies are responsible to their boards. The laws establishing the agencies clearly create the management structure. It creates the positions of Managing Director, Chairman, and Executive Vice Chairman, Director General as Chief Executive Officer, as well as Executive Directors or Commissioners and assigns responsibilities to them.

The boards report to the supervising minister. This could be through a director in the ministry designated to oversee the activities of the agency, or through the permanent Secretary of the ministry. The minister serves as a link between the agency and the president. The minister sometimes side-steps these two offices and deals with the regulatory agencies directly. There are a handful of regulatory agencies that the Acts setting them up empowers the president, through the minister to oversee to their specific and general operations.

The President sometimes relates informally and directly with the Chief Executives of key agencies. In this instance, the president may issue direct instructions that are of either specific or general in nature to the chief executive. This is usually the case with some grade A agencies.

Two offices within the presidency also serve as bridge between the president and the ministers. They are the secretary to the government of the federation, SGF and Head of civil service of the federation, HOS. The two play important roles in the reporting line between the regulatory institutions and the presidency. The third office within the presidency that also indirectly deals with the regulatory agencies is the chief of staff to the president. We will come to this later, but let's carry out adescription of the first two offices.

Adegoroye (2015) outlines that the functions and responsibilities of the Secretary to the Government of the Federation is mainly to coordinate and monitor implementation of government policies and programmes; and serve as think thank and technical backbone of the presidency.

Its specific functions include coordinating policy design and implementation by Ministries, Extra-ministerial Departments and Agencies for approval of government, coordinate the activities of ministries and government agencies on the implementation of government's decisions, policies and programmes and handling constitutional, political and socio-economic matters as maybe referred to the presidency.

Adegoroye goes ahead to describe the Secretary to the Government of the Federation as the number one diplomat in the country. His office connects the President to the bureaucracy, and the occupant ensures bureaucratic support for the president.

Appointments into the management and board of regulatory agencies by the President are coordinated and processed by the secretary to the government of the federation. He acts like the clearing house for that purpose. Most lobbyists for such position usually besiege the office of the Secretary to the government of the federation. Announcements for such appointments also come from the office. This does not however underplay the fact that the President may source for appointees using other channels.

The essence of making the SGF to coordinate federal appointment is to ensure proper record keeping, meeting federal character requirements and ensure religious and other parochial balance. The heterogeneous nature of Nigeria makes it very imperative.

The SGF signs the letters of appointment of all political appointees including the ministers and heads of regulatory agencies, while the president signs the letter of appointment of the chief of staff and secretary to the government of the federation.

There are however some instances where a minister supervising a parastatal would influence and determine such appointments, by making recommendations to the president, especially with parastatals that are technical in nature, or those whose Acts stipulates that nominations should come from some professional bodies to the president for approvals. This sometimes led to conflict between the SGF and the Minister in question.

The SGF relations and communications with the regulatory agencies are mostly in form of supervision and coordination of policy and programme implementation. The president's power of oversight of regulatory agencies is exercised largely through the SGF and sometimes, through the supervising minister. No wonder then that CEO's of regulatory agencies are regular visitors to the office of the SGF.

Another office that serves as a bridge between the regulatory agencies and the president is the office of the head of civil service of the federation, HOS.Adegoroye (2015) highlights its mandate as to provide effective leadership for the Civil Service and foster its professional development through career progression and development that engender creativity and motivate officers to enable them render public service with competence, objectivity and integrity, and to uphold at all times the public trust.

The HOS also provides professional leadership and direction to the civil service, maintains high ethical standards in the service, and continuously improves service-wide operational systems and performance standards of the service through reforms, training and counsel on the modernization of facilities and coordinates industrial relation matters of the civil service.

The HOS relates with regulatory agencies less than the SGF does. The role of the office is more on issues of management of staff discipline, ethical and professional conducts and observance of rules, regulations and processes of administration and public service. For instance, a staff of a regulatory agency having issues with its management may send a petition to the HOS for advice and direction. It is the responsibility of the HOS to interpret extant public service rules and communicate same to the management of the agency.

The president may also direct the HOS to investigate and deal with such issues involving top management staff of the regulatory agencies brought to his attention.

Another important office within the presidency whose function links it with regulatory institutions is the Chief of Staff to the President, COS.

Adegoroye (2015) says its main responsibility is to coordinate the deployment and management of state house resources and talents to manage the time and space of the president to enable him performs state duties in the most efficient manner on a sustainable basis.

The COS coordinates and controls all correspondences from the regulatory agencies to the president, and vice versa. This could be in form of executive orders and presidential directives. It also manages meetings between the president and CEO's and top management of the agencies. The office of the COS is so important that most times, board members and management of the regulatory agencies rarely see the president but end up picking presidential instructions from the COS and relaying responses through the same office.

The complex nature of Nigeria's politics, its dynamics and prominence given to a patronage system have led to situations where the chief of staff to the president acts outside stipulated duties, usurps the powers of other offices and assumes a different role in the country's power equation. The enormous powers the constitution confers on the president rubs off so much on his Chief of Staff, who takes advantage to expand his own power base. The allegation of abuse of office incumbent is a case in point.

Powers, functions, responsibilities and influence attached to other positions within the presidency are usurped by the chief of staff. This applies to the control of, and relations with the regulatory agencies. I spoke to a Former Secretary to the Government of the Federation in

Nigeria and he lamented how after his assumption of duty, he found himself in a supremacy battle with the president's chief of staff.

The COS either by his own initiative or acting on directives of the president serves as an alternative eye and ear of the president in the operation of the federal bureaucracy. Most presidents understand the need for an alternative source of information, monitoring and evaluation of projects, policies and programmes of government bureaucracy and parastatals. The COS sets up a shadow cabinet within his office for this purpose, manned by the different assistants to the COS.

Their functions and operations are also complemented by those of special advisers, senior special assistants and personal assistants to the president. They usually meet periodically under the COS to appraise situations. This arrangement further exacerbates the rivalry within the presidency as CEOs of regulatory agencies develop some bonds and royalty to them in the course of their interactions.

ChiefExecutives of regulatory agencies who by structure are supposed to report to the SGF resort to the Chief of Staff to the president upon their realization of the enormous powers and influences of the office. This distorts the established arrangement, and it comes with implications. The SGF serves as institutional memory for the federal government in terms of appointments and policy directives. This maybe lost to a Chief of Staff that usurps the powers of the SGF.The SGF issues and documents all executive orders, more commonly referred to as circulars within the public service in Nigeria. There could be inconsistencies if another office carries out the responsibilities.

Rivalries within the bureaucracy are common across the world, but also pronounced in Nigeria. That between the president's appointees, such as the SGF and COS as I have outlined above is no exception. The President is best placed to eliminate or reduce such rivalry and power tussle as it affects the performances and efficiency of regulatory agencies. Reporting lines are not straight; flow of directives is dispersed, and the agencies do get multiple and conflicting instructions on policy and programme issues.

A strong and dominant president reduces this problem, but a weak one enhances such power play.

What Nigeria needs is a strong political office to solely coordinate and supervise the operations of all regulatory agencies in the country. The Secretary to the Government of the federation, SGF is best suited for this role. As I pointed out earlier, the constitution already saddles the SGF with this role. Struggle for power and influence as well as unnecessary supremacy battle has seen other offices, especially within the presidency usurp some of the SGF roles.

It is incumbent largely on the President and to a lesser extent on the National Assembly through its investigative and oversight powers to insist that the right things be done.

Reforming Economic Regulatory Framework: The South Korean Example

For Nigeria to quickly realize the need for urgent and radical reform of its regulatory system, it is imperative for the country to look up to another country that it shares similarities with and at the same time has navigated through a transformation of its own economic regulatory system. It is in the light of this that we will in this chapter, look at what South Korea did that threw it up as a global reference point.

South Korea, one of the countries referred to as Asian Tigers is a classic example of systematic reforms of economic regulatory system that aligns with existing reality. It has the 11th largest economy in the world by 2016 and the 4th largest in Asia with a GDP of 1.411 trillion US Dollars according to the World Bank.

Its economy has experienced one of the largest transformations of the past 60 years. Kim, (1991) is of the view that the Korean economy started as agriculture based in the 1960's. The economy however had a quantum leap within decades to become of one the reference points across the developing world.

Daeyong, (2001) attributes the series of reform programmes that turned around the Korean economy to the 1997 economic crisis that hit the country. The crisis, according to him, resulted from structural weaknesses accumulated in a state-led economic development of past three decades. The new government, he said faced a critical time to take urgent actions for economic recovery.

The government initiated drastic regulatory reform programs in parallel with structural reforms in four sectors: finance, corporate, public and labour. They were all aimed to promote the efficiency and discipline using market principle and market force. These reform measures in a broad sense included changes in regulatory systems and methods, and policy tools. Far-reaching efforts at reform of regulation were conducted.

A strong political leadership combined with a sound institutional framework for regulatory reform made it possible to carry out drastic and comprehensive reform of regulation.

> According to a report of a South Korean Presidential Commission on regulatory reforms, the former government of President Kim, Young-Sam in 1993 launched government reforms responding to this demand. At that time, government reform drives focused on administrative simplification and deregulation on business activities, reflecting the progress of democratization and economic liberalization. To do so, several reform bodies, such as the Presidential Commission on Administrative Reform, the Economic Deregulation Committee, the Industrial Deregulation Committee and Meeting on Regulatory Reform were established from 1993 to 1997.

These reform bodies were on the *ad hoc* and advisory basis. The Presidential Commission on Administrative Reform dealing with a wide range of reform issues including deregulation was the most active. All members of the Commission were composed of civilian experts from university professors, economic researchers, media, trade union and civic group. It was a good model to establish a partnership with the private sector in conducting government reform. However, its authority depended on political influence rather than on a legislative authority. A sound institution for regulatory reform was not established yet.

The report also stated that the Korean government enacted a law known as the Basic Act on Administrative Regulations, BAAR Actin 1974, drawn largely from experience and lessons from government reforms of the past that focused on reinforcing the weakness of the fragmented approach to economic regulatory reforms in the past. The Act philosophy is rooted on the need to pursue market driven regulations suitable for a global environment by replacing command and control manners with market competition.

It puts more focus on adjusting relations between the state, market, and civil society, and deals with regulation imposing obligation or restriction on laws and subordinating rules such as presidential decree, ministerial ordinance, notice and instruction.

Change of government in 1998 did not affect the implementation of the new law. The president set implementation targets for cabinet ministers. In overall, the plan resulted in eliminating 5, 430 and improving 2, 411 out of 11,125 regulations in place at the time and submitted 344 bills for implementation to South Korean National Assembly in 1988. 321 of the bills were passed same year.

Further in-roads were made in 1999 with the elimination of 503 regulations and another 570 revised. 51 additional bills were submitted to the National Assembly with 43 of them passed.

The Korean government also established a central registration system for regulations in the country to manage the stock of regulation in the country. According to the Korean government white papers on Regulatory reforms in 1999 and 2000, ministries were required to register regulations under their jurisdiction. It should include content of regulations, legal authority and agency responsible for it.

This arrangement provided a good data base for regulatory management that is open and accessible to both the public and government on the internet site www.rrc.go.kr. It provided a platform where information is shared on the issue of regulation and in the process, transparency is enhanced. For regulations to be enforceable, the regulatory agency must first be registered in the data base.

Another significant feature of the Korean economic regulatory system is its tenure basis. Regulations are effective for a five-year period, after which renewals can be granted with the necessary compliance and approvals.

In line with the Korean regulation reforms, informal regulations such as codes, rules and administrative fiats not based on appropriate legal authority were eliminated. Over 1,678 of such items were eliminated. The rule is that all regulations must flow from proper legal and legislative authority.

There are several lessons Nigeria can draw from the South Korean experience. The two countries share a lot in common considering their economic development trajectory and challenges. While South Korea navigated through the tough terrain to become one of the largest economies in the world, Nigeria is still battling with basic economic problems.

I earlier noted that Nigeria has been unable to embark on a systematic reform of its economic regulatory framework. There is every need for a reset of the regulatory system in line with the Korean model.

Most of present-day regulatory agencies in Nigeria were created during the Obasanjo administration. The administration was in a hurry to reform the country's inefficient and nearly comatose public sector. Credit must be given to the far-reaching reforms it introduced. But, the pressure to achieve a lot and promptings by Breton woods institutions led to fast-tracking of the reforms process.

The government in 2001, through the Bureau of Public Enterprise, BPE, set up a steering committee on competition and anti-trust reforms in Nigeria, as part of the haste to ensure that the necessary regulatory institutions were put in place against the background of private sector intrusion into the country's economy.

Wilson, (2005) however notes that the mandate and terms of reference of the committee included preparation of draft legislation to eliminate monopolies, remove restrictive conduct and foster competition in all economic sectors and establish a regulatory agency for each sector. This was however not achieved, forcing the government to adopt a half-hazard approach to the building of regulatory institutions in the country.

The problem continued with the lawmakers. The absence of the legislative arm of government during the period of military dictatorships thwarted and stunted its development. It has been struggling to institutionalize the business of law-making since the restoration of democracy in 1999.

The result was a legislature that was most times cajoled into doing a wishy-washy job on the bills without due diligence and necessary scrutiny. The output, just as the initial weak bills that were sent, is also weak and lacking in legal thoroughness that blocks loopholes and ensures smooth enforcement of the provisions of the acts.

Despite attempts to put an effective regulatory framework in place in Nigeria, gaps, weaknesses, contradictory roles and in some cases absence of a regulatory institution for some critical sectors of the economy still characterize the existing situation in the country. I mentioned in previous chapters how the ports sub-sector of the larger marine sector in Nigeria is enmeshed and mired in controversy and confusion.

There have been rivalry and supremacy contests among agencies operating in the sector as to who has what regulatory powers. This rivalry has been dragged to the courts for the interpretation of the regulatory roles of the different agencies.

It took a judgment of the appeal court in Nigeria to resolve the contention overwhether the Nigeria Shippers Council is a regulatory institution for terminal operators in Nigeria's maritime sector. As Iriepken (2018) reports, the court in its judgement on March 15, 2018, in a case between ENL consortium LTD, and the federal government, the Bureau of Public Enterprises, and the Nigeria Ports Authority declared that the Nigeria Shippers Council was an economic regulator in the maritime industry in Nigeria.

This is clearly an indication of the haze that surrounds Nigeria's economic regulatory system.

CHAPTER SIX

A Compendium of Regulatory Agencies in Nigeria

This book would not be deemed complete without a comprehensive list and major objectives of regulatory institutions in Nigeria. This would be done on ministry to ministry basis,

Ministry of Environment

- National Environmental Standards Regulation and   Enforcement Agency, NESREA.

NESREA has responsibilities for the protection and development of the environment, biodiversity, conservation and sustainable development of Nigeria's natural resources in general and, technology including coordination and liaison with, relevant stakeholders within and outside Nigeria on matters of enforcement of environmental standards, regulations, rules, laws, policies and guidelines.

Its vision is to ensure a cleaner and healthier environment for Nigerians. Its key functions include the enforcement of compliance with laws, guidelines policies and standards on environmental matters. It also includes coordinating and liaising with stakeholders, within and outside Nigeria on matters of environmental standards, regulation and enforcement.

It also enforces compliance with provisions of international agreements, protocols, conventions and treaties on environment, including climate change, biodiversity, conservation, desertification, forestry, oil and gas, chemicals, hazardous wastes, ozone depletion, marine and wild life pollution, sanitation, and such other environmental agreements as may from time to time come into force.

NESREA headquarters office is located at 4 Oro-Ago Crescent, Off Mohammed Buhari Way, Garki, Abuja.

- National Oil Spill Detection and Response Agency, NOSDRA.

NOSDRA was established by the National Assembly Act of 2006 as an institutional framework to coordinate the implementation of the National Oil Spill Contingency Plan, NOSCP for Nigeria, in accordance with the international convention on oil pollution preparedness, response and cooperation, OPRC to which Nigeria is a signatory.

It also ensures compliance with environmental legislations in the Nigerian petroleum sector. It liaises with relevant stakeholders in the Nigerian Oil and Gas industry to evolve methods of environmental management to cope with the dynamics of the Petroleum sector.

Its functions include to identify high risk areasas well as priority areas for protection and clean up and ensure a programme of activation, training and drill exercise to ensure readiness to oil pollution preparedness.

Its vision is to create, nurture and sustain a zero tolerance for oil spill incidents in the Nigeria environment.

The Agency's corporate headquarters is located on the 5th floor, NAIC house, plot 590, zone AO, central business district, Abuja.

- Environment Health Officers Registration Council of Nigeria, EHORCON.

The specific objectives of EHORCON include determining what standards of knowledge and skills are to be attained by persons seeking to become members of the profession of environmental health and improving those standards from time to time as circumstances may permit.

Its functions include:
- Improve and protect human health from environment hazards
- Enforce environment health regulations
- Develop liaison between the inhabitants and local authority, and between local authority and higher authority
- Act independently to provide advice on environment health matters
- Initiate and implement advocacy and health promotion and education programmes to promote an understanding of environment health principles.

Its vision is to position environment health practice as the fulcrum of public health.

EHORCON head office is at 15 M.L. Wushishi Crescent, Off OkonjoIweala Way, Utako, Abuja.

- The National Biosafety Management Agency, NBMA.

NBMA was established by the National Bio-safety Management Agency Act 2015, to provide regulatory framework to adequately safeguard human health and the environment from potential adverse effects of modern biotechnology and genetically modified organisms, while harnessing the potentials of modern biotechnology and its derivatives, for the benefit of Nigerians.

Its mandate is to promote biotechnology development in all sectors of the Nigerian economy. It is also to promote indigenous acquisition and development of easy and affordable requisite technology in Nigeria and indigenous Rand D to generate copious innovations in biotechnology, as well as for the sustenance and growth of the biotech industry.

The Agency regulates modern biotechnology activities and the release into the environment, handling and use of genetically modified organisms which are products of modern biotechnology to prevent adverse impact on the environment and human health.

Its vision is to promote the basic tenets of bio-safety as enunciated in the Cartagena Protocol on biosafety and enforce Nigeria National Bio-safety Management Act of 2015.

The office is at Umaru Musa Yar' Adua Express way, near old City Gate, National Park Service, Abuja.

Ministry Of Trade and Investment

- Consumer Protection Council, CPC.

CPC was established by Act no 66 of 1992. It commenced operations in 1999. Its mandate requires it to eliminate hazardous products from the market, provide speedy redress to consumer complaints, undertake campaigns that will lead to consumer awareness, ensure that customers interests receive due consideration at the appropriate forum, and encourage trade, industry and professional associations to develop and enforce in their various fields quality standards designed to safeguard the interests of consumers.

It also has the mandate to eliminate the scourge of consumer rights abuses in the Nigerian market place by educating consumers on their rights and how they could be protected. The Council also acquaints businesses of their obligations to customers.

Its core functions include:

- Providing speedy redress to consumer complaints through negotiation, mediation and conciliation
- Removing hazardous products from the market and causing offenders to replace such products with safer and more appropriate alternatives
- Publishing from time to time the list of products whose consumption and sale have been banned, withdrawn, severally restricted or not approved by the federal government
- Causing an offending company, firm, trade association or individual to protect, compensate, provide relief and safeguards to injured consumersor communities from adverse effects of technologies that are inherently harmful
- Undertaking campaigns and other forms of activities that will lead to increased consumer awareness
- Encouraging trade, industry and professional associations to develop and enforce in their various fields quality standards
- Encourage the formation of voluntary consumer groups or associations for consumer wellbeing
- Ensuring that consumer interests receive due consideration at appropriate fora and providing redress to obnoxious practices or the unscrupulous exploitation of the consumers by companies, firms, trade associations or individuals
- Registering and monitoring products, services and sales promotions in the market place.

The vision of the Consumer Protection Council is to be a dynamic, effective and responsible apex consumer protection Agency of the Federal Government of Nigeria, championing the cause of fully sensitized consumers to achieve a caring and consumer-friendly community.

Its head office is located at 105 Dar Es Salam Street, Off Aminu Kano Crescent, Wuse 2, Abuja.

- Standards Organization of Nigeria, SON.

SON was established by an Act in 1979 to ensure the preparation of standards relating to products, measurements, materials and processes amongst others, and their promotion at the national, regional and international levels.

It carries out the certification of industrial products and helps in the production of quality goods and improvement of measurement accuracy and circulation of information relating to standards.

SON also advises the federal government generally on national policy on standards, standards specification, quality control and metrology, designating, establishing and approving standards.

The functions of the Organization include:

- Designation, establishment, approval and declaration of standards in respect of metrology, materials, commodities, structures and processes.
- Certification of products in commerce and industry throughout Nigeria.
- Quality control of products, weights and measures.
- Matters relating to metrology- ensure reference standards for calibration and verification of measures and measuring instruments
- Investigation of quality of products etc.
- Enforcement of standards.
- Quality management.
- Registration and regulation of standard marks and specifications etc.
- Establishment and maintenance of laboratories.
- Compilation and publication of scientific or order data.
- Sponsoring national and international conferences.
- Proffering professional advice to government of the federation or state on specific problems relating to standards specifications.
- Research.
- Establishment of standard library.

Its corporate headquarters is at 52 Lome Crescent, Wuse Zone 7, Abuja.

- Corporate Affairs Commission, CAC.

CAC was established by the Companies and Allied Matters Act, which was promulgated in 1990 to regulate the formation and management of companies in Nigeria.

The commission was mandated to deal with perceived inefficiency and ineffectiveness of the erstwhile company registry, a department within the Federal ministry of commerce and tourism which was then responsible for the registration and administration of the repealed Companies Act of 1968.

Its functions include:

- The regulation and supervision of the formation, incorporation, management and winding up of companies
- To establish and maintain companies' registry and offices in all the states of the federation, suitably and adequately equipped to discharge its functions under the Act or any law in respect of which it is charged with responsibility
- Arrange and investigate the affairs of any company where the interests of the shareholders and public so demand
- To undertake such other activities as are necessary or expedient for giving full effect to the provisions of the Act establishing the commission

Its vision is to be a world class company's registry providing excellent registration and regulatory services.

The headquarters is located at Plot 420, Tigris Crescent, Off Aguiyi Ironsi street, Maitama, Abuja.

- Financial Reporting Council of Nigeria, FRCN.

FRCN has the responsibility of oversight and ensures quality in accounting, auditing, actuarial valuation and corporate governance standards and non-financial reporting issues in organizations in Nigeria.

Its functions include:

- Protect investors and other stakeholders' interests
- Give guidance on issues relating to financial reporting and corporate governance to professionals, institutional and regulatory bodies in Nigeria

- Ensure good corporate governance practices in the public and private sectors of the Nigerian economy
- Harmonize the activities of relevant professional and regulatory bodies as relating to corporate governance and financial reporting
- Promote the highest standards among auditors and other professionals engaged in the financial reporting process
- Enhance the credibility of financial reporting
- Improve the quality of accountancy and audit services, actuarial, valuation and corporate governance standards

Its vision is to be the conscience of regulatory assurance in financial reporting and corporate governance in Nigeria.

The main office is at LCCI Conference centre, 10, Olowopopo street, Near MKO Abiola Gardens, Central Business District, Alausa, Lagos.

Ministry of Power

- Nigeria Electricity Regulatory Commission, NERC.

NERC was established by the power sector reform Act of 2005 to undertake technical and economic regulation of the Nigerian electricity supply industry.

The Commission is to, among others, license operators, determine operating codes and standards, establish customer rights and obligations and set cost reflective industry tariffs.

The commission has the mandate through appropriate regulations, to ensure that the nation gets adequate, reliable and affordable services in the generation, transmission, distribution and trading of electricity.

The commission is also entrusted with the responsibility of ensuring the participation of the private sector in the electricity market. The commission ensures that regulations which encourage profitable pricing and effective competition among market players are developed and implemented. It also ensures that appropriate codes of conduct and rules of engagement are also enforced to ensure an efficient and investor-friendly market. It is also mandated to monitor industry operators and prevent abuse of the market power.

The commission is also charged with ensuring consumers fulfil their obligation by paying for power used and their interests protected. In discharging this responsibility, NERC will develop, in consultation with licenses, customer service standards, fair pricing rules and facilitate constant communication with consumers, to ensure they understand their rights and obligations.

The commission is also to ensure and establish an effective dispute resolution mechanism to guarantee consumer protection. It shall also ensure that it is even-handed in the regulation of the industry and must be firm and fair in the enforcement of rules and regulations.

The vision of NERC is electricity on demand, while its corporate headquarters is at Adamawa Plaza, plot 1099. First Avenue, off Shehu Shagari Way, central business district, Abuja.

- Nigeria Electricity Management Services Agency, NEMSA.

NEMSA, formerly the Electricity Management Services Limited, EMSL is one of the successor companies established by the federal government in line with relevant laws. In line with the provisions of NEMSA Act 2015, it is mandatory that all electrical installations in power plants/stations, transmission and work places where electricity is used, as well as all electric meters and instruments to be deployed in electricity environment, are to be inspected, tested and certified fit and safe by electrical inspectors of NEMSA and the NEMSA National Meter test stations before they can be used in Nigeria.

Other responsibilities of NEMSA include

- To carry out technical inspectorate services for the Nigerian electricity supply industry
- Enforce all statutory technical electrical standards and regulations as published by the Nigerian Electricity Regulatory Commission and all other statutory bodies
- Collaborate with standards organization of Nigeria and other relevant government agencies to ensure that all major electrical materials and equipment used in Nigeria are of the right quality and standards
- Ensure that the power systems and networks put in place have been properly executed before use, to ensure that such installed systems can deliver safe, reliable and sustainable electricity supply to consumers nationwide
- Process and issue competency certificates to qualified electrical personnel working in the Nigerian electricity supply industry

- Regularly carry out periodic inspection, monitoring and assessment of existing power plants or stations, installations, extra high voltage and high voltage transmission lines, associated transmitting or switching stations and distribution networks to ensure that they are in regular fitness to generate, transmit, distribute and deliver reliable and safe power supply to electricity consumers nationwide
- Promote research on matters affecting the generation, transmission, distribution and utilization of electricity.

The vision of NEMSA is to be an efficient world class technical enforcement agency that ensures standardization, specification, quality, safety, and competence for the competitive Nigerian electricity supply industry and other allied industries.

Its headquarters is at 4 Dar-Es-Salaam Crescent, Off Aminu Kano Crescent, Wuse 2, Abuja.

Ministry of Education

- Joint Admission and Matriculation Board, JAMB.

JAMB was established by Decree no 2 of 1978 and amended in 1988 with the responsibility of ensuring a uniform standard for the conduct of matriculation examinations for entry into all universities, polytechnics and colleges of education in the country, and to place suitably qualified candidates in the available spaces in these institutions.

It also has the mandate to appoint examiners, moderators, invigilators, members of subject panels and committees and other persons with respect to matriculation examination and any other matters connected with it.

In placing suitably qualified candidates in the tertiary institutions, JAMB will take the following into account.

- Vacancies available in each institution
- Guidelines approved for each tertiary institution by the proprietors or other competent authorities
- The preference expressed or otherwise indicated by the candidates for certain tertiary institutions and courses
- Collate and disseminate information on all matters relating to admissions into tertiary institutions or any other relevant matter to the discharge of the functions of the board

JAMB, apart from the conduct of unified tertiary matriculation examination, UTME, also creates admission requirements for students seeking entry into tertiary institutions in the country,

- National Commission For Colleges Of Education, NCCE

The NCCE was established by Decree, (now Act) 13 of 1989 (Amended Act 12 of 1993 as a completion of the tripod in the supervision of higher education in the country. Its main function is to make recommendations on the national policy necessary for the full development of teacher education and training of teachers in Nigeria.

It also has the responsibility of laying down minimum standards for all programmes of teacher education and accrediting their certificates and other academic awards after obtaining thereof, prior approval of the minister of education.

It also has the mandate to approve guidelines setting out criteria for accreditation of all colleges of education in Nigeria. It also determines the qualified teachers' needs of Nigeria for the purpose planning facilities and prepare periodic master plans for the balanced and coordinated development of colleges of education.

Other function of the NCCE is the harmonization of entry and duration of courses at the colleges of education, collate, analyse and publish relevant information relating to teacher education in Nigeria, advise on, and take measures to improve immediate and long term prospects of technical and business education teachers, with respect to status and remuneration, and provide encouragement for women to enter a wide range of pre-vocational courses in technical education.

- Teachers Registration Council, TRC.

TRC was established by Decree (now Act) 31 of 1993. Several decades of agitation by professional teachers and other stakeholders for the establishment of a regulatory agency led to the enactment of the Act.
It registers and licenses qualified teachers in the country. It also accredits, monitors and supervises courses and programmes of teacher training institutions in Nigeria to ensure that they meet national and international standards.

The institution includes the colleges of education, faculties and institutes of education in Nigerian universities, schools of education in the polytechnics and the National Teachers Institute.

The council also organizes internship schemes and induction programmes for fresh education graduates to equip them with the necessary professional skills before licensing them for full professional practice.

It also enforces professional ethics among teachers using teachers' investigative panel and teacher's tribunal.

The council is charged with the following responsibilities:

- Determining who qualifies as a teacher in Nigeria.
- Determining what standards of knowledge and skills are to be attained by persons seeking to become registered teachers and raising those standards from time to time as circumstances permit.
- The establishment and maintenance of a register of teachers and publication from time to time of the list of those persons
- Regulating and controlling the teaching profession in all its aspects and ramifications
- Classifying from time to time members of the teaching profession according to their level of training and qualification

The vision of TRC, is to control and regulate teacher education, training and practice at all levelsand sectors of the Nigerian education system, in order to match teacher quality, discipline, professionalism, reward and dignity with international standards.

- National Universities Commission, NUC

The NUC was established in 1962 as an advisory agency, but later transformed to a regulatory institution for universities in Nigeria. It approves all academic programmes Nigerian universities and grants approval for the establishment of all higher educational institutions offering degree programmes in Nigerian universities.

It also ensures quality assurance of all academic programmes offered in Nigerian universities and provides channel for all external support to Nigerian universities.

In addition, the NUC lays down minimum academic standards in universities and accredits their degrees and other academic awards. The regulatory body for universities in Nigeria also advises the president and state governors, through the minister and commissioner of education, on the creation of new universities and other degree awarding institutions in the country.

The goals of the National Universities Commission are
- Attainment of stable and crisis-free university system
- To foster partnership between the Nigerian university system for delivery of quality university education
- To match university graduate output with national manpower needs
- Upgrade and maintain physical facilities in the Nigerian university system

Its vision is to be a dynamic regulatory agency acting as a catalyst for positive change and innovation for the delivery of quality university education in Nigeria.

Ministry of Finance

- National Insurance Commission, NAICOM.

NAICOM was established in 1997 by the National Insurance Commission Act with the responsibility for ensuring the effective administration, supervision, regulation and control of insurance business in Nigeria, and protection of insurance policyholders, beneficiaries and third parties to insurance contracts.

It hopes to strengthen insurance institutions by creating an effective regulatory framework and to facilitate deeper market penetration in the insurance industry

Its core functions include:
- Establish standards for the conduct of insurance business in Nigeria.
- Approve rates of Insurance premiums to be paid in respect of all classes of insurance business
- Approve rates of commission to be paid in respect of all classes of insurance business
- Ensure adequate protection of strategic government assets and other properties
- Act as advisers to the Federal government on all insurance related matters
- Approve standards warranties applicable to all insurance businesses

- To publish for sale and distribution to the public, annual reports and statistics on the insurance industry
- Liaise with and advise federal ministries, extra ministerial departments, statutory bodies and other government agencies on all matters relating to insurance as contained in any technical agreements to which Nigeria is a signatory.

Its vision is to be among the leading regulators of the insurance sector in the emerging market.

- Securities and Exchange Commission, SEC.

The origin of the Securities and Exchange Commission dates to 1962 when an ad hoc consultative advisory body, known as Capital Issues Committee was established under the aegis of the Central Bank of Nigeria. Its mandate was to examine applications from companies seeking to raise capital from the capital market and recommend the timing of such issues to prevent issues clustering which could over stretch the market's capacity.

Securities and Exchange Commission came into being following the promulgation of Decree No 71 of 1979 and was given powers to regulate and develop the Nigerian capital market, in addition to determining the prices of issues and setting the basis for the allotment of securities. Its powers were enhanced by a new Act known as The Investment and Securities Act No 45 of 1999.

The commission has powers to regulate and develop the Nigerian capital market, in addition to determining the prices of issues and setting the basis for the allotment of securities.

It also carries out the registration of securities and market intermediaries to ensure that only fit and proper persons/institutions operate in the market. The commission also carries out inspection and audit of any participant in the capital market.

It also carries out surveillance on exchanges and trading systems to forestall breaches of market rules as well as deter and detect manipulations and trading practices which may cause market disruptions.

The Securities and Exchange Commission is also mandated to mediate between parties involved in a dispute in the capital market.

Its vision is to be Africa's leading capital market regulator.

Presidency

- Central Bank of Nigeria, CBN.

The Central Bank of Nigeria is the regulatory institution for banks and other financial institutions in the country. The nature of role played by the bank has however been severally modified by the different amendments to the law establishing it. It will be difficult to list the Central Bank as being under the presidency as the 2007 amendment act guarantees its autonomy. Despite the autonomy, the bank has continued to report to the presidency.

The Central Bank Act of 1958, the Banking Decree of 1969, the Banks and Other Financial Institutions (BOFI}Decrees 24 and 25 of 1991, the CBN Amendment Decree No 3 and BOFI (Amended) Decree No 4 of 1997 and the CBN Act of 2007 were the laws that shaped the operations of the apex bank in Nigeria in terms of autonomy and scope of operations.

The current legal framework within which the CBN operates is the CBN Act of 2007, it provides that the Bank shall be a fully autonomous body in the discharge of its functions with the objective of promoting stability and continuity in economic management, promoting stability and continuity in economic management, ensuring monetary and price stability as well as rendering economic advice to the federal government.

In addition, the CBN is saddled with the responsibility of managing monetary policy in the country, regulation and supervision of banks, as well as non-financial institutions.

The vision of the CBN is to be proactive in providing a stable framework for the economic development of Nigeria, through effective, efficient, and transparent implementation of monetary and exchange rate policy, and management of the financial sector.

- Independent National Electoral Commission, INEC,

INEC was established in accordance with section 153 (f) of the 1999 Nigerian Constitution to, apart from conducting elections in the country, register and regulate the activities of political parties. It is also charged with monitoring of political campaigns and providing rules and regulations governing political parties.

The commission is expected to be guided by the following values in the performance of its duties.

- Carry out all functions independently, free from external control and influence
- Display openness and transparency in all its activities
- Provide level playing field and fairness

The vision of INEC is to be one of the best election management bodies in the world that meets the aspiration of the Nigerian people.

- Public Complaints Commission, PCC

The Nigeria Ombudsman (Public Complaints Commission) is the machinery for the control of administrative excesses (non- adherence to procedures or abuse of law). It is an organ of the government set up to redress complaints lodged by aggrieved citizens or residents in Nigeria against administrative injustice.

The Commission aims at promoting social justice for the individual citizen. It is also to provide a viable option for Nigerians or anyone resident in Nigeria seeking redress against injustice arising from administrative bureaucratic errors, omission or abuse by officials of government, or limited liability companies in Nigeria.

The Commission also has the role of improving public administration in the laws, procedures, practices, rules and regulations and standard behaviour of officials. These are provided for in the ACT, CAP 37 LFN 2004.

The primary function of the Public Complaints Commission is to provide impartial investigation on behalf of the complainants who feel aggrieved by the action or inaction of the government or local government or private companies.

The Commission is independent of government bureaucracy and at the same time has extensive powers regarding confidentiality and access to all government information including the production of documents which can aid the Commission's investigation.

The Commission is empowered to enforce compliance in order to obtain the necessary information. This power is vital to the Commission in facilitating impartial investigation to arrive at a fair and equitable decision. Investigation of all complaints are provided at no cost to both the complainant and respondent i.e. citizen and non – citizen resident in the country and their complaints are treated with the confidentiality they deserve.

Its vision is to ensure just administrative practices in Nigeria, build a nation where no man is oppressed and to promote social justice in Nigeria.

• National Lottery Regulatory Commission, NLRC

The National Lottery Regulatory Commission was established through the National Lottery Act of 2005. The Commission was primarily born out of the need to regulate the operations of lottery business, promote transparency and accountability in lottery, and protect the interest of players, stakeholders and the public.

Its main functions are mainly to issue licenses and permits, set standards, guidelines, rules and promote transparency, integrity in the operations and business of lottery in Nigeria.

The commission is also mandated to carry out periodic assessment of the operation of lottery and submit report to the president and the National Assembly.

Another function of the commission is to ensure accurate monitoring and assessment of proceeds accruing to operators to determine the value of the 50% prize money, and ensure 20% contribution to the National Lottery Trust Fund in line with the mandate of the Commission

Its vision is to be a trusted regulator of lotteries for good cause in national development.

• Nigeria Atomic Energy Commission, NAEC.

NAEC was established and activated in 2006 following the promulgation of its act in 1976. It is Nigeria's focal energy agency charged with the responsibility for the promotion of the development of atomic energy and for all matters relating to the peaceful use of atomic energy.
Its mandate includes:
- Construct and maintain nuclear installations for generating electricity
- Produce, use and dispose of atomic energy and carry out research into matters connected with the peaceful uses of atomic energy

- Manufacture or otherwise produce, buy or otherwise acquire, treat, store, transport, and dispose of any radioactive substances
- Plan with universities and other institutions or persons in Nigeria to conduct research into matters connected with atomic energy or radioactive substances
- Prospect for and mine radioactive minerals
- Educate and train persons in matters connected with atomic energy and radioactive substances
- Advise the federal government on questions relating to atomic energy. Its vision is to lay an enduring foundation for the building of a world class institution for peaceful development of nuclear technology in all its ramifications for national development, in conformity with international best practices, its head office is at 9 Kwameh Nkrumah Crescent, Asokoro, Abuja.

Ministry of Sports

- Nigeria Football Federation, NFF

The main objective of the Nigeria Football Federation is to constantly promote, regulate and control the game of football throughout the territory of Nigeria in the light of football unifying values of education, culture and humanitarianism.

The main objectives of the Nigeria Football Federation are as follows:

The main objectives of the Nigeria Football Federation is to constantly promote, regulate and control the game of football throughout the territory of Nigeria, in the light of football unifying values of education, culture and humanitarianism.

Broadly, the functions of the NFF are inclusive of the following:

Encourage the development of all forms of amateur and professional football in Nigeria
- Organize League and other matches for professional and amateur Clubs in co-operation with respective bodies recognized by the Federation

- Organize the participation of Nigerian Clubs in international competitions
- Provide, in co-operation with other bodies, adequate training for its employees and various personnel who may be involved in the administration and organization of League matches and its activities, with a view to improving the standard of football administration and organization.
- Determine such areas of league activities to be commercialized, in order to earn income for the League, the professional players, professional clubs and the federation
- Organize and regulate the activities of the Nigeria Referees Association (NRA) and grant annual licenses to persons taken to be Members of the NRA, to enhance the status of football referees
- Organize and grant annual licenses to persons taken to be members of the Nigeria Coaches Association

Ministry of Transportation

- Nigerian Maritime Administration and Safety Agency, NIMASA

The Nigerian Maritime Administration and Safety Agency (NIMASA) is the apex regulatory and promotional maritime agency. The Agency was created from the merger of National Maritime Authority and Joint Maritime Labour Industrial Council (former parastatals of the Federal Ministry of Transport) on 1st August 2006. The obligation of regulating the Maritime industry in Nigeria rests on the Agency through the relevant instruments: -

i. Nigerian Maritime Administration and Safety Agency Act. 2007.
ii. Merchant Shipping Act. 2007.
iii. Coastal and Inland Shipping (Cabotage) Act 2003

The Agency was established primarily for the administration of Maritime Safety Seafarers Standards and Security, Maritime Labour, Shipping Regulation, Promotion of Commercial Shipping and Cobatage activities, Pollution, Prevention and Control in the marine environment, the Agency also implements domesticated International Maritime Organizati on (IMO) and International Labour Organization (ILO) conventions.

108

Core Functions:

- Pursue the development of shipping and regulatory matters relating to merchant shipping and seafarers.
- Administration and regulation of shipping licenses.
- Administration, regulation and certification of seafarers.
- Establishment of maritime training and safety standards
- Regulation of safety of shipping as regards the construction of ships and navigation.
- Provision of maritime search and rescue services
- Provide direction and ensure compliance with vessels security measures
- Carry out air and coastal surveillance
- Control and prevent Maritime Pollution
- Develop and implement policies and programs, which will facilitate the growth of local capacity in ownership, manning and construction of ships and other maritime infrastructure.
- Enhance and administer the provision of Cabotage Act. 2003
- Perform port and flag state duties.
- Provide maritime security.
- Establish the procedure for the implementation of conventions of the International Maritime Organization (IMO) and the International Labour Organization (ILO), and other international conventions to which the Federal Republic of Nigeria is a party on maritime safety and security, maritime labour, commercial shipping, and for the implementation of codes, resolutions and circulars arising there from.

Its vision is to be the leading maritime administration in Africa advancing Nigeria's Global Maritime goals.

- Nigeria Ports Authority, NPA

Regulation of the Maritime sector in Nigeria has been enmeshed in controversy and has not well been clearly spelt out. There have been rivalry and supremacy contests among Agencies operating in the sector as to who has what regulatory powers. This rivalry has been dragged to the courts for the interpretation of the regulatory roles of the different Agencies.

The Act setting up the Nigeria Ports Authority empowers it to be an operator and a regulator. This maybe the source of the conflict within the sector.

The NPA, by its enabling Act should provide and operate, in the ports, such facilities as appear to it best calculated to serve the interest of Nigeria, maintain, improve and regulate the use of the ports.

It also ensures the efficient management of port operation, optimal allocation and use of resources, diversification of sources of revenue and guaranteeing adequate returns on its investments to contribute effectively to the well-being of the Nigerian society.

It is also charged with the responsibility to manage, supervise and control or take part in management, supervision, or control of any company undertaking in which the authority is interested by shareholding or otherwise.

It also controls pollution arising from oil or any other from ships using the port limits or their approaches; it also controls the erection and use of wharves in any port or approaches. It additionally provides, appoints, licenses and regulatesweighers and for measuring goods in any port in Nigeria.

- Nigeria Shippers Council, NSC

It took a judgment of the Appeal court in Nigeria to resolve the contention over whether the Nigeria Shippers Council is a regulatory institution for terminal operators in Nigeria's maritime sector. As Iriepken (2018) reports, the court in its judgment on March 15, 2018, in a case between ENL consortium LTD and the federal government, the Bureau of Public Enterprises, and the Nigeria Ports Authority declared that the Nigeria Shippers Council is an economic regulator in the maritime industry in Nigeria.

The Council is therefore mandated to create effective regulatory regime at the Nigeria ports for the control of tariff, rates, charges, and other economic services and to address the negative impact of port concession activities on the economy. Due to the absence of an economic regulator and to realize the optimal benefits of the federal government of Nigeria's port reforms processes.

The responsibility of the Council is to ensure efficient and timely delivery of shipping services to importers and exporters by the shipping service providers under the most economical arrangement.

It also moderates and stabilizes costs (freight rates, port charges, local shipping charges, haulage charges etc.) it is also supposed to give regular and reliable advice to the federal government on matters affecting the shipment of goods to and from Nigeria.

Its vision is to be the foremost economic development agency providing regulatory system that fosters efficient, effective and competitive service delivery in the transport sector.

Ministry of Science and Technology

- Energy Commission of Nigeria, ENC.

ECN came into being because of the action of the heads of state of Economic Community for West African States (ECOWAS) at their meeting in 1982 in Conakry, Guinea leading to adoption of a declaration that a body to be called Energy Commission of each member state should be established and charged with the responsibility of coordinating and supervising all energy functions and activities within each member state. The Energy Commissions are expected to link up with the African Energy Commission on behalf of their respective countries.

The role of the Energy Commission of Nigeria is the overall planning, coordination and effective direction of the formulation and implementation of national energy strategies and plans.

It is intricately linked to the functions and programmes of activities of various ministries, NGOs, as well as international organizations.

Its major objectives include:

- Guarantee increased contribution of the energy sector to national income and the economy
- Guarantee adequate, sustainable and optimal supply of energy at appropriate cost and in an environmentally responsible manner to the various sectors of the economy, by utilizing all viable energy resources in an optimal mix
- Promote an efficient consumption pattern of energy resources

111

- Promote indigenous acquisition of energy technology and managerial expertise, as well as indigenous participation in the energy sector industries
- Promote increased investments and development of the energy sector industries with private sector participation.

The functions of the Energy Commission of Nigeria are energy policy and planning, policy strategies, coordination and monitoring of the performance of the energy sector, training, research and development, and advising federal government on the funding of energy research, development, production and distribution.

Its vision is to ensure adequate, reliable, cost-effective and sustainable energy supply for the nation's economic and socio-political development. Its address is at Plot 701c, central business district, Abuja.

- Nigeria Institute Of Science Laboratory Technology, NISLT

The act establishing the institute came into existence in 2003, with the regulation, management and maintenance of institutional and industrial laboratory technologies in Nigeria as its core mandate. It is also saddled with the responsibility of advancing science laboratory technology profession in Nigeria.

Its other functions include determining the standard knowledge, exposure to equipment, practical and skills to be attained by persons seeking to become registered members of the profession and reviewing those standards from time to time as circumstances may require.

It is also required to promote the highest standards of competence, practice and conduct among the members of the profession, securing the establishment and maintenance of a register of members of the profession and its periodic publication.

The institute is also mandated to conduct examinations and granting certificates and diplomas and advising on, assisting in examinations relating to science laboratory technologists through the council.

Its vision is to cause rapid development of the nation through science laboratory technology.

Ministry of Justice

- National Human Rights Commission, NHRC.

The National Human Rights Commission of Nigeria was established by the national human rights commission Act 1995 (as amended) in line with Resolution 48/134 of the United Nations General Assembly which enjoins all member states to establish independent National Institutions for the promotion, protection and enforcement of human rights. The commission serves as an extra-judicial mechanism for the enhancement of the respect for and enjoyment of human rights. It also provides avenues for public enlightenment, research and dialogue to raise awareness on human rights issues.

The commission, realizing that human rights campaign cannot be achieved solely through the development of protective laws or establishment of mechanisms to implement those laws, engages in series of educational and public enlightenment programmes to raise public awareness on human rights issues.

It deals with all matters relating to the protection of human rights as guaranteed by the constitution and other international charters. It monitors and investigates all alleged cases of human rights abuses and violations and makes appropriate recommendation to the president for prosecution and any other action as maybe deemed necessary.

The commission regularly holds workshops, seminars, conferences and interactive sessions with relevant stakeholders. The commission has also engaged in continuous media advocacy and periodic publications aimed at disseminating appropriate human rights messages.

Sensitization, education and enlightenment programmes have also been carried out by the Commission in collaboration with NGOs and CBOs, to raise awareness on human rights throughout the country. Village Square meetings are also held across the country to discuss the mandate of the commission and other issues of relevance to specific local environments

- Nigeria Copyright Commission, NCC.

There have been some laws regulating copyright in Nigeria, but the birth of the Nigeria Copyright Commission was in 1988 when former military president, Ibrahim Babangida approved the establishment of the commission. The Copyright Council was inaugurated in 1989 with the sole mandate for the administration, protection and enforcement of all matters of copyright in Nigeria.

It has powers of enforcement and of apprehending copyright offenders. It monitors and supervises Nigeria's position in relation to international conventions and advises government on international agreements. The commission also develops and formulates regulations for the printing and publishing industry. It further develops and formulates the Nigerian Copyright Mediation Rules as an Alternative Dispute Resolution mechanism

The Copyright Commission also has the responsibility to inform and enlighten the public on matters relating to copyright. It also maintains an effective data bank on authors and their works.

The Commission has powers to receive and grant application for compulsory license and is vested with powers of approving and registering for operation, a collecting society.

Its vision is to harness the potentials of creativity for national development.

Ministry of Mines and Steel Development

• Council of Nigerian Mining Engineers and Geoscientists, COMEG

COMEG is the regulatory body for all professionals and firms in the geosciences, mining, engineering and metallurgy in the country. It was established through Act No 40 of 1990.

Its major thrust is to regulate the practices of professionals in the fields of geology, geophysics, geochemistry, mining engineering, petroleum engineering, metallurgy, etc. These professionals through their practices contribute over eighty percent of Nigerian foreign exchange earnings annually.

Its regulatory responsibilities are targeted at the extractive industries, which undoubtedly constitute the backbone of the nation's economy.

COMEG is charged with the responsibility of prescribing and enforcing the standards of education and experience for persons to practise as professionals in the extractive industries. It also registers, regulates and controls the practices of the professionals listed earlier.

Its vision is to ensure professionalism through education and regulation of practices in the Nigerian extractive industries.

Ministry of Aviation

- Nigerian Civil Aviation Authority, NCCA

NCCA was established by Decree 49 of 1999 with the statutory responsibilities of ensuring, regulating, monitoring and promotion of the safety, security, economic and reliability of air navigation oversight in line with international civil aviation organization, ICAO. NCCA effectively commenced operations on 1st January 2000.
Specifically, the NCCA has the following responsibilities
- Regulation of safety of aircraft operations, air navigation and aerodrome operations
- Monitoring of aircraft operating environment for safety and security
- Regulating of methods of entry and conduct of air transport business
- Advising the ministry of aviation on policy formulation on aviation related matters
- Balancing the economic interest of operators, users of aviation services as well as the public and the nation as a whole
- Setting of aviation training standards and approval of training institutions
- Facilitating take-off and operations of E-ticketing and billing settlement plan.
Its vision is to be one of the leading civil aviation authorities in the world.

Ministry of Petroleum Resources

- Petroleum Products Pricing Regulatory Agency, PPPRA

PPPRA is saddled with the responsibility of regulating the supply and distribution of petroleum products across the country. It was established with the mandate to, in consultation with other stakeholders in the downstream sector of the petroleum industry, determine the pricing policy of petroleum products in the country.

It also carries out the function of creating information data bank through liaison with all relevant agencies to facilitate the making of informed and realistic decisions on pricing policies. It also oversees the implementation of the relevant recommendations and programmes of the federal government as far as petroleum products supply and distribution are concerned.

The PPPRA also dwells on the moderation of volatility in petroleum products prices, while ensuring reasonable returns to operators. It establishes parameters and codes of conduct for all operators in the downstream petroleum sector.

The agency also maintains constant surveillance over all keys indices relevant to pricing policy and periodically approves benchmarks and prices for all petroleum products.

The agency equally is involved in the business of identifying macro-economic factors with relationship to prices of petroleum products and advises the federal government on appropriate strategies for dealing with them.

Other functions of the PPPRA are preventing collusion and restrictive trade practices harmful in the sector, creating firm linkages with key segments of the Nigerian society and exercising mediatory role as necessary for all stakeholders in the industry.

Its vision is to attain a strong, vibrant downstream sub-sector of the petroleum industry, where refining, supply and distribution of petroleum products are self-financing and sustaining.

- Department Of Petroleum Resources, DPR

DPR has the responsibility of ensuring compliance to petroleum laws, regulations and guidelines in the oil and gas industry. The discharge of these responsibilities involves monitoring of operations at drilling sites, producing wells, production platforms and flow stations, crude oil export terminals, refineries, storage depots, pump stations, retail outlets, and any other location where petroleum is stored or sold, and all pipelines carrying crude oil, natural gas and petroleum products.

The Department is also saddled with the responsibility of supervising all petroleum industry operations being carried out under licenses and leases in the country.

It also monitors petroleum operations to ensure that they are in line with national goals and aspirations including those relating to flare down and domestic gas supply obligations.

The Department also ensures that health, safety and environment regulations conform with national and international oil field practice. It maintains records of petroleum industry operations, particularly on matters relating to petroleum reserves, production exports, licenses and leases.

Another of the function of the regulatory agency is advising government and relevant government agencies on technical matters and public policies that may have impact on the administration of petroleum activities.

The Department processes industry application for leases, licenses and permits, ensures timely and accurate payments of rents, royalties and other relevant dues to government, and maintains and administers the national data repository.

Its vision is to be a leading regulator in the oil and gas sector.

- Nigerian Nuclear Regulatory Authority, NNRA

The Nuclear Safety and Radiation Protection Act 1995 established the Nigeria Nuclear Regulatory Authority with the responsibilities for nuclear safety and radiological protection regulation in Nigeria.

In specific terms, the Authority regulates radiological protection and nuclear safety to ensure the protection of life, health, property and the environment from the harmful (effects of ionizing)radiation and ensures safety and security of radioactive sources and nuclear materials and, to enable Nigeria meet its international obligations on the peaceful uses of nuclear technology.

Other functions of the Authority are:
- Sets and documents clear requirements, using a process that includes consultations
- Promotes compliance with regulatory requirements
- Verifies that processes and programmes satisfy regulatory requirements
- Consults with stakeholders when establishing priorities, development policies and planning programmes and services

- Regulates persons, organizations and practices that are subject to the Act establishing it, in a manner that is consistent with the risks posed by the regulated practice

Its vision is emplacement of the best regulatory control regime for all activities involving ionizing radiation and nuclear energy.

- Nigeria Content Development And Monitoring Board, NCDMB

NCDMB was established by the Nigerian Oil and Gas Industry Content Act of 2010 to maximize Nigeria's oil and gas activities.

Its key thrust is to integrate oil-producing communities into the oil and gas value chain, foster institutional collaboration, maximize utilization of Nigerian resources and attract investments to the Nigeria oil and gas sector.

The board also reviews, assesses and approves Nigerian content plans developed by operators and sets guidelines and minimum content levels for project related activities across the oil and gas value chain.

It is also charged with the responsibility of engaging in targeted capacity building interventions that would deepen indigenous capacities- human capital development, infrastructure and facilities, manufactured materials and local supplier development.

The regulatory institution has the mandate to grow and manage the Nigerian content development fund and monitor Nigerian content compliance by operators and service providers.

It also conducts studies, research, investigation, workshops and trainings aimed at advancing the development of Nigerian content.

Its vision is to be the instrument for the industrialization of Nigeria.

Ministry of Lands, Housing and Urban Development

- Architect Registration Council Of Nigeria, ARCON

ARCON was established by decree No. 10 of 1969 with the mandate to register and control the practice of architecture in Nigeria. It maintains a register of architects and architectural firms in the country. It issues certificates of professional competence to those whose names appear on the register.

The council also determines what standards of knowledge and skill are to be attained by persons seeking to become members of the architect profession and raises those standards from time to time as circumstances may permit.

It also approves and accredits courses of training intended for persons who are seeking to become, or are already qualified as architects.

The council also disciplines members with the establishment of a disciplinary tribunal and an investigating panel to hear cases.

- Council of Registered Builders of Nigeria, CORBON

The Council of Registered Builders of Nigeria was established by Decree No. 45 of 1989. It is a body empowered to regulate the practice of building construction, maintenance, and management in Nigeria.

It regulates and controls the practice of building profession in all its aspects and ramifications, including conducting professional accreditation of tertiary academic institutions and training facilities for the building profession.

It seeks to promote excellence in the building technology profession as well as to influence construction policies in Nigeria.

The body also conducts professional examinations and interviews for those who are aspiring to qualify to practice the building profession in Nigeria and ensures maintenance of discipline within the profession. It also registers would be professionals.

Its vision is to be a vibrant, reputable council that is discharging its mandates, advancing the interests of the building technology profession.

- Estate Surveyors Valuers Registration Board Of Nigeria, ESVRBN

The Board was established by Decree No. 24 of 1975 and charged with the responsibility of regulating the practice of estate surveying and valuation in Nigeria.

It determines the membership of the profession, standards of knowledge and skills to be attained by persons seeking to be registered as estate surveyors and valuers and reviewing such standards from time to time for the purposes of raising them.

It also maintains a register of persons entitled to practise as estate surveyors and valuers and its periodic publication.

The Board operates a tribunal to disciplines members that violate the codes and regulation of the profession.

The board also accredits courses relating to estate surveying run by tertiary institutions in Nigeria.

- Town Planners Registration Council Of Nigeria, TOPREC

The Council was established by Decree No. 3 of 1988 to regulate and control the practice of town and physical planning in all its aspects and ramifications.

It is entrusted with the responsibility of ensuring that only thorough-bred professionals are accredited, registered and eligible to practice the profession.

The Council determines those to be involved in the profession and sets standards of skills and knowledge to be attained by persons seeking to become members of the profession. It also establishes and maintains a register of persons entitled to the practice of the profession.

In addition, the Board, in accordance with the law, maintains appropriate conduct, discipline and order within the profession.

Ministry of Works

- Council For The Regulation Of Engineering In Nigeria, COREN

COREN was established by Decree 55 of 1970 and amended by Decree 27 of 1992 as a statutory body to regulate the practice of engineering in Nigeria.

Apart from regulating the practice of the profession and training of professionals, COREN also enforces the registration of all engineering personnel.

The main objectives are to ensure that the practice of engineering in Nigeria is in accordance with relevant codes of practice in the interest of public safety and are carried out by qualified Engineering personnel.

The Council ensures and puts in place continuing professional development programmes for Engineers in the country and also investigates and disciplines members in breach of professional codes and regulations.

- Surveyors Registration Council Of Nigeria, SURCON

SURCON was established by Decree 44 of 1989 to regulate the practice of surveying in Nigeria.

The Council determines who qualifies as professional surveyors in Nigeria, the standard of knowledge and skill to be attained by persons seeking to become registered as members of the profession of surveying.

The regulatory agency also secures the establishment and maintenance of a register of persons entitled to practise the profession. It also regulates and controls the practice of the profession in all its ramifications, while also maintaining discipline within the profession.

Ministry of Agriculture

- Veterinary Council of Nigeria, VCN

VCN is charged with the responsibility of coordinating and overseeing the practice of the veterinary profession in Nigeria. This includes determining what standards of knowledge and skills are to attain by persons seeking to be registered as veterinary surgeons and raising standards from time to time as circumstances may permit.

The council is also empowered to establish and maintain a register of persons registered from time to time. It serves more as a quality assurance organ for the veterinary sector in the country.

The council also gives approval to Veterinary schools for the training of veterinary surgeons after ensuring that they have the requisite human and material infrastructure. It also monitors such approved schools to ensure that standards are not only being maintained but are also improved upon.

The regulatory body conducts registration examinations in respect of candidates who did not pass through approved schools, but whose curriculum council believes may offer adequate training.

- Nigeria Agricultural Quarantine Services, NAQS

NAQS is a regulatory agency created for the harmonization of plants, veterinary and aquatic resources (fisheries) quarantine in Nigeria. It is also expected to promote and regulate sanitary (animal and fisheries health) and phytosanitary (plant health) measures about the import and export of agricultural products, with a view to minimizing the risks to agricultural economy, food security and the environment.

The main objective of NAQS is to prevent the introduction, establishment and spread of animal and zoonotic diseases, as well as pests of plants and fisheries including their products.

The service also undertakes emergency protocols to control or manage new pest incursion or disease outbreak in collaboration with key stakeholders.

It also ensures that Nigeria's agricultural exports meet with international standards in line with International Plant Protection Convention, IPPC and other global bodies.

Another of its mandate is to ensure that all plants, animals and aquatic products and produce leaving the shores of the country through all exit points, meet international standards as specified by International Plant Protection Convention.

Its vision is to be the leading regulatory agency responsible for the prevention of introduction and or spread of exotic pests and diseases of all agricultural products in international trade.

Ministry of Information, Culture and Tourism

• National Film and Video Censors Board, NFVCB

NFVCB was established as the regulatory agency for the film and video sector of the Nigerian economy. It is empowered to classify all films and videos whether imported or produced locally.

It is also the duty of the Board to register all films and video outlets across the country and to keep a register of such outlets.

The goals of the Board include the provision of enabling environment for the growth of the film industry, manage the classification system to time, cost, and quality standards, and provide policy advice and services to government.

Its functions include, but not limited to licensing a person to exhibit films and video works, regulate and prescribe safety precautions to be observed in licensed premises, and to regulate and control cinematographic exhibitions.

Other functions of the board are monitoring and enforcement activities to curb the release of unapproved movies into the market, institute stringent sanctions against the violators and institute reward mechanisms to produce positive themed movies, such as advance production grants, lower censorship charges for advocacy films.

Its vision is to be recognized as a world-class film and video regulatory agency that institutes best practices in the discharge of its duties.

- National Broadcasting Commission, NBC

The National Broadcasting Commission is vested with the responsibility of regulating and controlling the broadcasting industry in Nigeria. Its other responsibility is advising the federal government on the implementation of the National Mass Communication Policy, as it relates to broadcasting, as well as licensing all categories of television and radio services.

It also undertakes research and development in the broadcast industry, upholding the principles of equity and fairness in broadcasting and establishing and disseminating a national broadcast code while also setting standards with regards to the contents and quality of materials broadcast.

The Commission also receives processes and considers application for establishment, ownership or operation of radio and television licenses. It also receives, considers, and investigates complaints from individualsand corporate organizations regarding the contents of a broadcast station and the conduct of a broadcast station.

It is also charged with the mandate to promote Nigerian indigenous cultures, moral and community life through broadcasting, determining and applying sanctions, including revocation of licenses of defaulting stations, which do not operate in accordance with the broadcast code and in public interest, and approval of transmitter power, location of stations, areas of coverage as well as regulate types of broadcast equipment to be used.

- Nigerian Press Council, NPC

The Nigerian Press Council was established by Act No. 85 of 1992 to ensure the maintenance of high professional standards for the Nigerian press. One of its major functions therefore is to enquire into complaints against the press from the public and into complaints from the press about the conduct of persons or organization towards the press. Simply put, the council serves as a buffer between the press and the public and advice on measures

The council monitors the activities of the press with a view to ensuring compliance with the code of professional and ethical conduct of the Nigeria Union of Journalists, researches into contemporary press development and engage in updating press documentation.

Other functions of the council include review of developments likely to restrict the flow of information advise on measures aimed at remedying such developments, review of media laws, policies and programmes or developments perceived as hostile to the press in its performance and advise on possible remedy.

The council is also saddled with the responsibility of protection of the rights and privileges of journalists in the lawful performance of their duties and monitoring the performance of the print media to ensure that owners and publishers comply with the terms of their mission statements and objectives in liaison with the Newspaper Proprietors Association of Nigeria. (NPAN)

- Advertising Practitioners Council Of Nigeria, APCON

APCON was established by Act No. 55 of 1988, a move that accorded deserved state legislative recognition of advertising as a profession in Nigeria and vested the council with powers to regulate and control the practice of advertising in the country in all its ramifications.

Its main objective is to promote responsible and ethical advertising practice, acts as the conscience of society in matters of commercial communications and as a watchdog for consumers.

It also manages the needs and interests of stakeholders in Nigeria advertising industry.

APCON cooperates with sectoral associations in regulating the conduct of their member organizations to ensure a socially responsible practice. It checks all forms of abuses in commercials such as misleading statements, spurious testimonials, visual and verbal exaggeration, misleading offers, suggestion or pictures offensive to public decency by insisting on pre-exposure clearance of all advertisements.

Ministry of Water Resources

- Nigeria Integrated Water Resources Management Commission, NIWRMC

NIWRMS was established in 2007 to control and regulate the right by all persons to develop and use water resources shared by more than one state. It seeks to rationalize and streamline possible indiscriminate development, use, diversion of, and regulation of water affecting more than one state.

It also facilitates and synergizes the activities of all stakeholders and provides conflict resolution mechanisms and platforms to resolve disputes amicably.

The commission's other functions include the implementation of regulatory policies on activities relating to the development of water resources in Nigeria, be responsible for economic and technical regulation of all aspects of water resources exploitation and provision of public and private water resources infrastructure, ensuring the safety and quality of water services by regulating standards for execution and performance, and issuance of water resources licenses in accordance with the provisions of the Act.

The commission also monitors the conduct of holders of licenses and enforces its conditions, reports charges paid by consumers to the minister, liaises withrelevant agencies to conduct studies and surveys for establishing water resources balance, catchment management plans and water efficiency strategies.

Its vision is to be a world class water resources regulatory agency in Nigeria, ensuring sustainable delivery of sufficient quantity and quality water for all uses.

Ministry of Health

- Medical and Dental Council of Nigeria, MDCN

MDCN is charged with the responsibility of regulating conduct of medical and dental practitioners in Nigeria. Its powers were enhanced by Decree No. 23 of 1988.

The council determines the standards of knowledge and skill to be attained by persons seeking to become members of the medical or dental profession and reviews those standards from time to time.

It secures the establishment and maintenance of a register of persons entitled to practice as members of the medical or dental profession. The council also prepares and reviews code of conduct for the practice of medicine and dentistry.

The Council also supervises and controls the practice of homeopathy and other forms of alternative medicine in Nigeria. It also makes regulation for the operation of clinical laboratory practice in the field of pathology, clinical cytogenetics, haematology, medical microbiology and parasitology and medical virology.

Its vision is to be the foremost professional regulatory body in Nigeria.

- Institute of Chartered Chemist of Nigeria, ICCN

Decree No. of 1993 established the Institute of Chartered Chemist of Nigeria. Its mandate is to regulate the teaching and standard best practice of Chemistry in the country.

It carries out this mandate by establishing and maintaining a register of Chartered Chemists in Nigeria and raising the standards as the situation may warrant. It is also responsible for professionalizing the practice of Chemists by exercising regulatory authority and control over all persons in private or public or public organizations and corporate bodies handling all chemicals.

It also establishes standards and regulations about chemical production, usage and management, and reviewing such standards from time to time.

The institute, in conjunction with educational institutions in Nigeria, standardizes chemistry educational curricular in secondary and tertiary levels, it is also responsible for information/data collation, processing and dissemination about chemical usage and management to stakeholders and government authorities for policy formulation.

The institute audits the quality of personnel in chemical related manufacturing outfits to ensure conformity with standards.

The vision of the Institute is to recreate situations around us that would impact positively on the nation, while providing professional protection to members.

- Nursing and Midwifery Council of Nigeria, NMCN

The Nursing Council of Nigeria was established by the British colonial government to regulate and control the education and practice of the profession in Nigeria in 1947. Decree No. 89 of 1979 brought together other nursing regulatory bodies in the country under one council.

It is the only legal and administrative, corporate and statutory body charged with specific functions to regulate the nursing and midwifery profession and education in the country.

Its core objectives are to ensure high quality of nursing and midwifery education in Nigeria, maintain high standard of professional nursing and midwifery practice and enforce discipline within the profession. The councils' other functions include designing, implementing and evaluating various nursing and midwifery educational programmes, of indexing, examination, registration, certification, licensure of professional nurses and midwives and monitoring standards of nursing and midwifery practice in Nigeria.

Its other functions are to accredit all training institutions and clinical practice areas utilized for the education of all categories of nurses and midwives in Nigeria, conduct professional examinations for all categories of nurses and midwives in the country, and conduct and promote research in relevant areas of nursing and midwifery.

Its vision is to maintain professional ethics and etiquette and the quality of nursing care to clients and patients properly guaranteed.

- Radiographers Registration Board of Nigeria, RRBN

The Radiographers Registration Board of Nigeria was established by Decree No. 42 of 1987 to regulate and standardize the practice of radiography in the country.

The objective is to ensure the availability and provision of quality radiography services to Nigerians. The board ensures quality training programmes and seeks to regularly improve upon them through well-coordinated training, monitoring and inspection activities.

They work to provide quality manpower, ensure good working environment and guarantee job satisfaction. The Board is charged with the responsibility of determining the standard of knowledge and skill to be possessed by persons seeking to become members of the profession and to improve those standards.

It is also required to maintain a register of members of the profession and publication of same from time to time and conducting examinations in the profession and issuing certificate or diplomas to successful candidates as appropriate.

Its vision is to position radiography at the top of health profession in Nigeria.

- Medical Laboratory Science Council of Nigeria, MLSCN

MLSCN was established by Act 11 of 2003 to regulate medical laboratory services through registration and licensing of medical laboratories as well as practitioners, mandatory inspection, mentoring for quality improvement, accreditation, monitoring and evaluation as well as certification of laboratory test kits and reagents.

The Act also empowers the council to regulate the training of medical laboratory scientists, technicians and assistants.

It is also charged with the responsibility of evaluating, assessing and registration of foreign graduates of medical laboratory science.

Its vision is to be a world acclaimed regulatory agency driving the culture of quality and efficient health laboratory care to the public and ensuring high academic standards in training institutions.

- Institute of Public Analysts of Nigeria, IPAN

The institute was established in 2004 as a professional regulatory body with mandates to train, examine, register and regulate the practice of public analysts and analytical laboratories in Nigeria.

A public analyst is a registered member of the institute who by virtue of his or her knowledge, training, skill, competence and integrity is authorized by law to analyse consumer and health-related products such as food, drugs, medical devices, cosmetics, water, chemicals and biologically-based consumer products and issue certificates regarding their composition, use, quality, safety and efficacy.

The institute seeks to attain international standards such that export products would not only compete favourably in the global market, but also impact positively on our economy.

Its vision is to develop excellent professional scientific analysts who would act as catalysts for the industrial development of Nigeria as well as practices that would attain international reference status in the analysis of consumer products for the health and economic wellbeing of mankind.

- Health Records Officers Registration Board Of Nigeria, HRORBN

HRORBN was established by Decree No. 39 of 1989 to regulate the practice of health records keeping in Nigeria, by determining what standards of knowledge and skills shall be attained by a person seeking to become a member of the profession of health records management and improving those standards from time to time.

The board is also saddled with the responsibility of securing, in accordance with the Act establishing the Board, the establishment and maintenance of a register of persons registered under the Act as members of the profession, and the publication from time to time a list of these persons.

The board also conducts examination in health records management and awards certificates or diplomas to successful candidates as appropriate, and for such purpose the board shall prescribe fee to be paid.

Its vision is to establish a culture of excellence in health information management practices. education, training and research.

- Community Health Practitioners Registration Board of Nigeria, CHPRBN

The board was established by Decree No. 61, of 1992 to regulate community health practice in Nigeria. It determines the standards of knowledge and skills tom be attained by persons seeking to become members of the profession of community health and improving the standards from time to time.

It also establishes and maintains a register of persons involved in the profession and conducts examination in the profession, while awarding certificates of diploma to successful candidates.

The board indexes trainees for various community health practice courses and inspects schools and institutions where community health practitioners are trained for accreditation of community health programmes.

The board also organizes and conducts studies, seminars and workshop to upgrade knowledge and skills of community health professionals.

- Medical Rehabilitation Therapist Registration Board Of Nigeria, MRTRBN

MRTRBN was established by Decree No. 38 of 1988 to regulate the medical rehabilitation therapist profession in Nigeria.

It determines what standards of knowledge and skills are to be attained by persons seeking to become registrants of the relevant profession. It also raises standards from time to time as circumstances may permit.

It also conducts examination in the relevant profession and awards degree or diploma certificates to successful candidates as appropriate and the regulation and control of professional practice of physiotherapy, occupational therapy, speeches therapy and audiology in Nigeria either hospital based or otherwise.

It also accredits academic and clinical programmes for medical Rehabilitation training and practice in the country. The board also infiltrates discipline and decorum into the profession and eliminates quackery.

- Dental Technologists Registration Board Of Nigeria, DTRBN

The dental technologist registration board of Nigeria has the responsibility of regulating the practice of dental technology in the country.

It determines what standards of knowledge and skills are to be attained by persons seeking to become members of the profession and improves those standards from time to time.

It also establishes and maintains a register of persons registered as members of the profession, and periodic publication of the register.

The board also conducts examinations in the profession and awards certificates or diplomas to successful candidates, as well as the fees to be charged.

- Pharmacist Council of Nigeria, PCN

The council is charged with the responsibility for regulating and controlling pharmacy education, practice and training in all aspects and ramification.

The council is responsible for registration and licensing of all pharmacists, pharmaceutical premises, (manufacturing, importation, distribution, wholesale, retail, hospital pharmacies) as well as issuance of permits to pharmacy technicians and registration and licensure of patent and proprietary medicine vendors.

It also determines what standards of knowledge and skill are to be attained by persons seeking to become pharmacists in Nigeria. It also establishes and maintains a register of pharmacists and ensures periodic publication. It also issues oaths and codes of ethics to pharmacists.

The council appoints inspectors to ensure the enforcement of the provisions of the law by inspecting and monitoring of premises where pharmaceutical endeavors take place.

The council is a also saddled with the responsibility of organizing mandatory continuing professional development for members.

Its vision is to effectively regulate and control the training and practice of pharmaceutical services provided through the instrumentality of capacity building.

- Optometry And Dispensing Opticians Registration Board Of Nigeria, ODORBN

ODORBN was established by Decree No. 34 of 1989 to regulate the optometry profession in Nigeria. It seeks to protect the public by providing world class regulatory, registration and educational services and high standards of education for optometrists.

Apart from licensing professionals in the industry, the Board also compiles, maintains and publishes a register of members.

Its vision is to be a world class-rated optometrists and dispensing opticians' registration and regulatory body ensuring that professionals are people with personal integrity with global competitive competencies.

- Dental Therapists Registration Board of Nigeria, DTRBN

DTRBN was established by Decree No. 81 of 1993 for the regulation, control and training and practice of dental therapy in Nigeria.

The board ensures the registration of practitioners maintains and publishes periodically a register for the purposes of identification of members.

The board has the responsibility of disciplining members who violate codes of conduct and ensures their professional development.

Ministry of Internal Affairs

- Nigeria Security And Civil Defence Corps, NSCDC

NSCDC was established by an Act of the National Assembly in 2003 to regulate the operations of private security guards in Nigeria. Among other things, the corps shall register private guard companies in the country, from time to time, inspect the premises of private guard companies, their facilities and approve same if it is up to standard.

1. It also supervises and monitors the activities of all private guard companies and register them for operations. It is also required to periodically organize workshops and training courses for private guard companies and seal up any private guard company which operates without valid license.

Bibliograpgy

Abhuere, J. (2015), Why privatization is not the answer. An article in The Nigerian Observer, August 8, 2015.

Abioye, O. and Onuba, I, (2017). Banks' non-performing loans hit 2tn, A report in The Punch newspaper, April 6, 2016.

Ackah, C et al, (2010), State-Business Relations and Economic Performance in Ghana, IPPG Discussion paper series 35, Available online at www.ipp,org,uk.

Adegoroye, G. (2015) Restoring Good Governance in Nigeria: The Civil Service Pathway. Lagos: Kachofo Publishers,

Aderinokun, K. Adeosun: Nigeria's Tax to GDP Ratio among lowest in the world. A report in ThisDay newspaper of April 23, 2017.

Agbamuche-Mbu, M. PPPs key to our desired infrastructure development. An article in This Day newspaper, September 13, 2016.

Ajayi, G. (1999), Internal politics of decolonization and emergence of neo-colonialism in post-independence Nigeria. In G Ajayi (ed): Critical perspectives on Nigeria's socio-political development in 20th century. Lagos: Stebak Books.

Ake, C. (1966), Democracy and Development in Africa. Washington: The Brookings Institution.

Ake, C. (1981)A Political Economy of Africa, New York: Longman.

An unpublished report containing the resolutions of a presidential retreat with the private sector on Friday, October 14, 2011. The report contained among other things the demand by members of the private sector, mostly owners and captains of industry that the President Jonathan Government should accelerate the concession of key public infrastructure.

Anakwue, A. (2015), The Nigerian Bourgeoisie and The Vision 20:2020 Economic Development Blueprint. A PhD Thesis published by the department of political science and international relations, University of Abuja.

Asem, F, et all, (2013) Private Sector Development and Governance in Ghana. A working paper adopted by the International Growth Centre.

Banwo and Ighodalo. (2016), Why Nigeria is Ripe for A Competition Law. An online publication on November 24, 2016 on the website www.banwo-ighodalo.com.

Beblawi, H. and Luciani, G. (1987) The rentier state, London: Croom Helm.

Bello, K. (2017), Nigeria: To be restructured or not to be restructured? An unpolished seminar paper.

Calabresi, S AndYoo, C. (2008) The Unitary Executive: Presidential Power from Washington To Bush. Fordham Law Review, Vol. 79.

Cushman, R. (1941), The Independent Regulatory Commissions. Washington: The Brookings Institution.

Dada, A. "CBN rejects Finance Ministers' call for interest rate cut...retains in benchmark rate at 14 percent. A report on The Punch newspaper, September 21, 2017.

Daeyong, C. (2001) A Radical Approach to Regulatory Reform in Korea. A paper presented in The Annual 2001 Conference of the American Society for Public Administration at Rutgers University, New Jersey, USA.

Dempsey S. (2013) Competition and Antitrust Laws. Institute of Air & Space Law, Mcgill University.

Dlakwa, D. H, (2006) South-south Partnership for Oil Exploration in the Yobe Valley, Nigeria. Paper presented at the 1stYobe State Economic Summit, Damaturu.

Domhoff, W. (1979) The Powers That Be: processes of ruling class domination in America, New York: Random House.

Garba, J. (1995) Fractured history: Elite shifts and policy changes in Nigeria, (Princeton: Sungai books.

Giddens, A. And Held, D (ed), (1982) Classes, Power, And Conflict: Classical and Contemporary Debates, Hound mill: Macmillan Press.

Goddard, R. et al, (1996) International Political Economy: State-Market Relations in the Changing Global Order, Colorado: Lynne Rienner Publishers.

Hawke C. and Middleton W. (2011), Understanding Antitrust Laws, Competition, and Their Impact on Our Lives. In Social Education 75(2) National Council for Social Studies, New York.

Helleiner, G. (1966), Peasant agriculture, government and economic growth in Nigeria. Yale: Yale University press.

Iriepken, D. Appeal Court: Regulatory Agencies Cannot Impose Fines without Recourse to Court, A Report in This Day Newspaper, April 21, 2018.

Iweala, O. (2012), Reforming the Unreformable: Lessons from Nigeria. `London: The MIT press.

Jonathan suspends Lamido Sanusi. A report by Vanguard Newspaper of February 20, 2014.

Jhingon, M, (2007) The Economics of Development and Planning, Delhi: Vrida Publishing Ltd.

Jiang, J, et all, (2007) Study on the China Model: An Analysis of Economic Development Path of China. Beijing, People's publishing House.

Kim, K. (1991) The Korean Miracle (1962-1980) Revisited: Myths AND Realities in Strategy and Development. Kellogg Institute working paper No. 166.

Leslie, l. (1960) The great Issues of Politics, New Jersey: Prentice Hall Inc.

Malo, Y. (2015), Re: Why privatization is not the answer. An article in The Nigerian Observer, August 8, 2015.

Marx, K. (1848) Manifesto of the communist party, Beijing, China: foreign language press.

M McKenzie, R, and Lee, D. (1991) Quicksilver Capital: How The Rapid Movement of Wealth Has Changed The World. New York: Free Press.

Michael, S. _ (2015), The nature and structure of the economy of pre-colonial Nigeria. An internet publication, www.academia.edu/17090984/the_nature_and_structure_of_the_pre -colonial_Nigeria.

Miliband, R. (1969) The State in Capitalist Society, London: Weidenfeld and Nicolson.

Muhammad, H. FG to shut down NERFUND over 17.5bn bad loans. A report in The Daily Trust Newspaper, Friday, October 6, 2017.

Mukherjee, S. And Ramaswamy, (1999) A History of Political Thought: Plato to Marx, New Delhi: Prentice Hall.

National Economic Centre for Economic Management and Administration. (2000), Structural Adjustment Programme in Nigeria: Causes, Processes and Outcomes, A revised technical proposal prepared by the Institute.

Nelson, B. (1996) Western Political Thought: From Socrates To the Age of History, New Jersey: Prentice Hall.

Nnoli, O. (1986), Introduction to politics. Enugu: SNAAP press ltd.

Ogbuagu, C.S.A, (1983), The Indigenization Policy: Nationalism or Pragmatism? An article in the African Affairs magazine, Volume 82, Issue 327, April 1, 1983.

Ogunjimi, S. (1997) Public Finance for Polytechnics and ICAN students. Niger, Leken Productions.

Ogunremi, G, (1996), Traditional Factors of Production in Pre-colonial Economy. In G. O. Ogunremi and E. K. Faluyi (ed), An Economic History of West Africa Since 1750. Rex Publications, 1996

Okigbo, P.(1993) Essays in the Public Philosophy of Development: Change and Crisis in the Management of the Nigerian Economy, Vol. 2, Enugu, Fourth Dimension Publishing Company Limited.

Okonj, E. "Finally, NCC, MTN reach truce." A report in the "Thisday newspaper, June 11, 2016.

Okojo-Iweala, N. (2018) Fighting Corruption Is Dangerous: The Story Behind the Headlines. London: MIT press

Olukoju, A. (2001) Nigerian ports: The Imperatives of Radical Reforms, In the Nigerian Economic Summit Group Economic Indicators Journal, July-September 2001. Vol 7, no 3. P12.

Olukoshi, A. (1993), The Politics of Structural Adjustment in Nigeria. Ibadan: Heinemann Educational Books.

Oserogho and Associates. (2015), Anti-trust and Competition Laws in Nigeria. An article published in Proshare Intelligence Investing website, www.proshareng.com on November 2, 2015.

Osinbajo signs 3 Executive Orders. Proshare Intelligent Investing online publication on Friday May 19, 2017 at the website www.proshareeng.com/news/doing-business-in-nigeria/osinbajo.

Percival, P. (2011) Who's in Charge? Does the President Have Authority over Regulatory Decisions? Fordham Law Review, Vol. 79, Issue 6, Article 2.

Peterside, A. (2013) Nigeria realized N400bn from electricity privatization. An interview with Vanguard newspaper of September 3, 2013.

Sanjour, W. "Why Regulatory Agencies Don't Work" An Article on the website, http://sanjour.info written on May 1, 2012.

See Vision 20:2020 Economic Development Blueprint.

See the Presidential Commission on Administrative Reform, 1997, *White Paper on Administrative Reform in the Civilian Government,* and the

Regulatory Reform Committee, 1999, *White Paper on Regulatory Reform in 1999.*

See the National Policy on Public Private Partnership

See the Infrastructure Concession Regulatory Commission Act, 2005.

Soludo, C. (2005) The political economy of sustainable democracy in Nigeria. The 5th Nigeria democracy day lecture delivered on May 29, 2005 in Abuja.

The World Bank. (2016) Bank credit to the private sector – country rankings. As published in Theglobaleconomy.com at its website, www.theglobaleconomy.com/rankings/Bank-_credit__to_the_private_sector, visited on October 1, 2017.

Tijani, M. "Adeosun, Manufacturers want CBN to cut interest rates." A news report on The Cableonline newspaper, September 20, 2016.

Wil Udo, B. "MTN-NCC fine: setting a dangerous precedence." An analysis in The Premium times online newspaper, March 8, 2016.

Ugwu, C. (2017) Stock market posts 2.97 Trillion gain in nine months. A report in The Daily Telegraph Newspaper of Monday, October 2, 2017.

Ujah, E. (2017) FG to sell DISCO's to new investors. A report in The Vanguard Newspaper, Thursday, October 12, 2017.

Umoren, R. (2001), Economic Reforms and Nigeria's Political Class. Ibadan: Spectrum books.

Usigbe, L."FG Terminates Lagos-Ibadan Expressway Contract: Julius Berger, RCC to CommenceImmediate Reconstruction." The Tribune Newspaper. Tuesday, November 18, 2012.

Van D B, (1998) The Immanent Utopia: New Jersey: PRINCETON

Vogel, S. (1996) More rules: Regulatory Reforms in Advanced Industrial Countries. Ithaka and London: Cornel University Press.

What are executive orders? Apublication by civic and economic literacy. An internet publication dated August 14, 2015 and viewed on Monday May 22, 2017 at the internet website www.informationstation.org/video/what-are-executive-orders.

Williams, S."Passenger Service Charge: Any Gain from The Bickering?Business Day Newspaper. Thursday, December 15, 2011.

Wilson, I. (2005) Enhancing Nigeria's Economic Development: A case for Institutional and Regulatory Reforms in Nigeria's Banking Secto. An article published in Mondaq, a web magazine downloaded at www.mondaq.com

World Bank. 2016. Doing Business 2016: Measuring Regulatory Quality and Efficiency. Washington, DC: World Bank Group. DOI:10.1592/978-1-4648-0667-4-

Worsnop, R. (1969), Federal regulatory agencies: fourth branch of government. Editorial research reports vol. 1, Washington DC CQ press

Yahaya, H. (2017) Buhari: 200,000 farmers get 43.9 Billion Naira loan, a report in the Daily Trust Newspaper, Monday, October 2, 2017.

Yar'Adua, M. An interview granted to Financial Times of London on May 19, 2008.

APPENDIX A

List of Public Enterprises Scheduled for Privatization for the Period 2000 To 2014.

S/N	ENTERPRISE/TRANSACTION	MODE OF SALE	DATE OF SALE	FGN HOLDING PRE – PRIVATISATION (%)	FGN HOLDING SOLD (%)	FGN HOLDING POST – PRIVATISATION (%)
1	ANAMBRA MOTORS MANUFACTURING COMPANY LIMITED (NTMC)	Core Investor	December 13, 2006	35	24	11
2	AYIP-EKU OIL PALM	Core Investor Sale	May 17, 2007	60	60	Nil
3	CENTRAL PACKAGES OF NIGERIA LIMITED	Core Investor	December 13, 2006	94.23	94.23	Nil
4	DAILY TIMES OF NIGERIA (DTN)	Core Investor Sale	June, 2004	100	100	Nil
5	FEDERAL SUPER PHOSPHATE FERTILIZER COMPANY	Core Investor Sale	Septembe, 2005	100	100	Nil
6	IHECHIOWA OIL PALM PLC	Core Investor	August 14, 2006	60	60	Nil
7	ORE-IRELE OIL PALM	Core Investor Sale	Septembe, 2004	60	60	Nil
8	LAFIAGI SUGAR COMPANY	Liquidation	August 24, 2007	100	100	Nil
9	LAGOS INTERNATIONAL TRADE FAIR	Concession	May 17, 2007	100	100	N/A
10	LEYLAND NIGERIA LIMITED	Revalidation of Sale	April, 2005	100	100	Nil
11	NAFCON	Liquidation	August, 2005	100	100	Nil
12	NATIONAL CLEARING AND FORWARDING AGENCY	Core Investor	August 14, 2006	100	100	Nil
13	NATIONAL TRUCKS MANUFACTURERS LIMITED	Core Investor Sale	December 2002	75	75	Nil
			April 2004	24	24	Nil
14	NIGERIA CEMENT PLC	Share sold to Institutional Investors on the floor NSE	October 2002	10.72	10.72	Nil

15	NIGERIA MACHINE TOOLS, OSHOGBO	Core Investor Sale	December, 2005	80	70	10
16	NIGERIA NEWSPRINT MANUFACTURING LIMITED (NNMC)	Liquidation	July 01, 2008	100	100	Nil
17	NIGERIA PAPER MILL JEBBA	Liquidation	June 13, 2006	100	100	Nil
18	NIGERIA SUGAR COY BACITA	Liquidation	October, 2005	19.7	19.7	Nil
19	ONIGBOLO CEMENT COMPANY, REPUBLIC OF BENIN	Core Investor	May 17, 2007	43	43	Nil
20	PEUGEOT AUTOMOBILE LIMITED (PAN)	Sale to existing Share holder	July 2004	35	35	10
		AMCON took over 79.31%	July 2013			3.43
21	SAVANNAH SUGAR COY	Core Investor Sale	December 2002	90	90	4.88
22	STEYR NIGERIA LIMITED (STEYR)	Core Investor	August 14, 2006	75	75	Nil
23	SUNTI SUGAR COMPANY	Liquidation	September 2005	100	100	Nil
24	TAFAWA BALEWA SQUARE	Concession	May 17, 2007	100	100	N/A
25	VOLKSWAGEN OF NIGERIA LIMITED	Core Investor Sale	October 2005	35	35	
26	NIGERIA REINSURANCE CORPORATION	Core Investor Sale	December 2002	100	68.52	31.48
27	NICON INSURANCE CORPORATION	Core Investor	October 2005	100	87.32	12.68
28	FSB INT'L BANK PLC (NOW FIDELITY BANK PLC)	Share Flotation	April 2001	100	100	Nil
29	INTERNATIONAL MERCHANT BANK LIMITED	Share Flotation	April 2001	70.66	70.66	Nil
30	NAL MERCHANT BANK PLC (NOW STERLING BANK PLC)	Share Flotation	April 2001	100	100	Nil
31	CAPITAL HOTELS PLC (NOW ABUJA SHERATON)	Core Investor Sale	October 2002	90.33	90.33	2
32	NICON HOTEL, ABUJA (NOW TRANSCORP HILTON)	Core Investor Sale	October 2005	100	100	12
33	NIGERDOCK NIGERIA LIMITED	Core Investor Sale	December 2001	100	100	Nil
34	NATIONAL AVIATION HANDLING COMPANY (NAHCO)	Public Offer of Shares at NSE	November 2005	60	60	20
35	CEMENT COMPANY OF NORTHERN NIGERIA	Core Investor Sale	July 2000	100	100	Nil

		Share Flotation	April 2001			
36	BENUE CEMENT COMPANY PLC (180,148,377 offer for sale)	Core Investor Sale	May 2000	35	35	Nil
		Share Flotation	October 2000			
37	WEST AFRICA PORTLAND CEMENT COY PLC (94,814,813 offer for sale)	Core Investor Sale	October 2000	100	100	Nil
		Share Flotation	January 2001			
38	ASHAKA CEMENT COMPANY PLC	Core Investor Sale	March 2001	71.81	71.81	Nil
39	FESTAC 77 HOTEL	Asset Sale	January 2002	100	100	Nil
40	ABUJA INTERNATIONAL HOTEL (NICON LUXURY)	Core Investor	August 14, 2006	99.49	99.49	Nil
41	NIGERIA HOTELS LIMITED – IKOYI HOTEL, LAGOS	Asset Sale	October 2002	100	100	Nil
42	NIGERIA HOTELS LIMITED – CATERER's COURT IKOYI LAGOS	Asset Sale	December 2002	100	100	Nil
43	NIGERIA HOTELS LIMITED: Houses NO. 8 & 9 Lease RD Ikoyi Lagos	Asset Sale	April 2009	100	100	Nil
44	NIGERIA HOTELS LIMITED Adult Section (Properties) Lagos	Asset Sale	April 2003	100	100	Nil
45	NPA QTRS, LAGOS	Asset Sale	October 2004	100	100	Nil
46	CENTRAL HOTEL KANO	Asset Sale	July 2004	100	100	Nil
47	AFRIBANK NIGERIA PLC	Share Flotation	June 2005	33	33	Nil
48	ASSURANCE BANK PLC	Core Investor Sale	March 2002	90	90	Nil
49	ELECTRIC METER COMPANY OF NIGERIA, ZARIA	Core Investor Sale	December 2002	100	100	Nil
50	CALABAR CEMENT COMPANY (CALCEMCO)	Liquidation	August 2002	46.6	46.6	Nil
51	ASEPL 202 (LEAD, ZINC, BARYTES, COPPER, SALT)	Mineral Concession	August 29, 2006	100	100	N/A

	OGOJA					
52	ASEPL 203 (LEAD, ZINC, BARYTES, COPPER, SALT) OGOJA	Mineral Concession	August 29, 2006	100	100	N/A
53	ENUGU BRICKS	Core Investor Sale	June 2005	100	100	Nil
54	EPL 13212 (TALC, GOLD, CASSITERITE, ATAKUMOSA, OYO STATE)	Concession	May 17, 2007	100	100	N/A
55	EPL 14000 (GOLD WAYA, YAURI, KEBBI STATE)	Mineral Concession	May 17, 2007	100	100	Nil
56	EPL 17222 (GOLD BUKKUYUM LG, ZAMFARA)	Mineral Concession	May 17, 2007	100	100	Nil
57	EPL 17224 (GOLD BUKKUYUM LG, ZAMFARA)	Mineral Concession	May 17, 2007	100	100	Nil
58	EPL 17227 (GOLD BUKKUYUM LG, ZAMFARA)	Mineral Concession	May 17, 2007	100	100	Nil
59	IBADAN BRICKS	Core Investor Sale	June 2005	100	100	Nil
60	IGUN GOLD DITRICT (ML 20501, ML 20507, ML 10904)	Mineral Concession	August 29, 2006	100	100	N/A
61	IKORODU BRICKS	Core Investor Sale	June 2005	100	100	Nil
62	IZOM BRICKS & CLAY PROJECT, IZOM, NIGER STATE.	Core Investor	March 17, 2007	80	80	Nil
63	KADUNA BRICKS	Core Investor Sale	June 2005	100	100	Nil
64	KANO BRICKS	Core Investor Sale	June 2005	100	100	Nil
65	KURU QUARRY JOS	Concession	September 2005	100	100	Nil
66	NIGERIA FELDSPAR/QUARTZ	Mineral Concession	August 29, 2006	100	100	N/A
67	NIGERIAN BARYTES MINING (ML 18706)	Mineral Concession	August 29, 2006	100	100	N/A
68	NIGERIAN KAOLIN PACKAGE (ML 5543, 11930, 5647, 1939 AND 4069)	Mineral Concession	August 29, 2006	100	100	N/A
69	NTAMP 1 GURUM JOS, PLATEAU STATE	Mineral Concession	August 29, 2006	100	100	N/A
70	NTAMP 2 RAFIN JAKI BAUCHI STATE	Mineral Concession	August 29, 2006	100	100	N/A
71	NTAMP 3 BANKE KADUNA STATE	Mineral Concession	August 29, 2006	100	100	N/A
72	OGBOYEGA 1	Concession	May 17, 2007	36	36	N/A
73	OGBOYEGA 11	Concession	May 17, 2007	36	36	N/A

74	OKABA COAL BLOCKS	Concession	May 17, 2007	100	100	N/A
75	SALE OF PEGSON CRUSHER AND 500 KVA GENERATING SET AT OKABA, KOGI STATE	Asset Sale	November 2006	100	100	Nil
76	SML 21301 (GOLD MAGAMI SHIRORO LG NIGER)	Concession	May 17, 2007	100	100	N/A
77	SML 21302 (GOLD MAGAMI SHIRORO LG NIGER)	Concession	May 17, 2007	100	100	N/A
78	SULEJA QUARRY (ASSET SALE)	Asset Sale	September 2005	100	100	Nil
79	DELTA STEEL COMPANY LTD	Core Investor Sale	February 2005	100	80	20
80	ALUMINIUM SMELTER COMPANY OF NIGERIA (ALSCON)	Willing Buyer/Willing Seller	October 2004	92.5	77.5	15
81	JOS STEEL ROLLING MILLS LTD	Liquidation	November 2005	100	100	Nil
82	KATSINA STEEL ROLLING MILLS LTD	Liquidation	November 2005	100	100	Nil
83	OSHOGBO STEEL ROLLING MILLS LTD	Liquidation	November 2005	100	100	Nil
84	APAPA CONTAINER TERMINAL	Concession	March 2005	100	N/A	100
85	APAPA TERMINAL 'A'	Concession	October 2005	100	N/A	100
86	APAPA TERMINAL 'B'	Concession	October 2005	100	N/A	100
87	APAPA TERMINAL 'C'	Concession	March 2005	100	N/A	100
88	APAPA TERMINAL 'D'	Concession	March 2005	100	N/A	100
89	APAPA TERMINAL 'E'	Concession	October 2005	100	N/A	100
90	CALABAR NEW PORT TERMINAL A	Concession	May 17, 2006	100	N/A	100
91	CALABAR NEW PORT TERMINAL B	Concession	October 2005	100	N/A	100
92	KOKO PORT	Concession	May 17, 2006	100	N/A	100
93	LILYPOND INLAND CONTAINER DEPOT	Concession	September 2005	100	N/A	100
94	ONNE FLT A	Concession	October 2005	100	N/A	100
95	ONNE FLT B	Concession	October 2005	100	N/A	100
96	ONNE FOT A	Concession	October 2005	100	N/A	100
97	PORT HARCOURT TERMAINAL 'A'	Concession	May 2005	100	N/A	100
98	PORT HARCOURT TERMAINAL 'B'	Concession	May 2005	100	N/A	100

99	SKYPOWER AVIATION HANDLING COMPANY (SAHCOL)	Core Investor (Willing Buyer, Willing Seller)	September 30, 2009	100	Nil	100
100	TIN CAN ISLAND PORT RORO TERMINAL	Concession	September 2005	100	N/A	100
101	TIN CAN ISLAND PORT TERMINAL 'A'	Concession	September 2005	100	N/A	100
102	TIN CAN ISLAND PORT TERMINAL 'B'	Concession	September 2005	100	N/A	100
103	TIN ISLAND PORT TERMINAL 'C'	Concession	September 2005	100	N/A	100
104	WARRI CANAL BERTH	Concession	May 17, 2006	100	N/A	100
105	WARRI NEW TERMINAL A					
106	WARRI NEW TERMINAL B	Concession	October 2005	100	N/A	100
107	WARRI OLD PORT TERMINAL B	Concession	October 2005	100	N/A	100
108	WARRI OLD TERMINAL A	Concession	October 2005	100	N/A	100
109	BAKER NIGERIA LIMITED	Private Placement	January 17, 2007	36	Nil	36
		Private Placement	January 17, 2007	36	Nil	36
110	SPDC Stallion House Lagos	Core Investor	December 2006	51	51	Nil
111	BAROIDS DRILLING CHEM. PRODUCTS NIGERIA LIMITED	Private Placement	January 17, 2007	36	36	Nil
		Private Placement	January 17, 2007	36	36	Nil
112	BAROIDS NIGERIA LIMITED	Private Placement	January 17, 2007	36	36	Nil
		Private Placement	January 17, 2007	36	36	Nil
113	DOWELL SCHLUMBERGER	Private Placement	January 17, 2007	36	36	Nil
		Private Placement		36	36	Nil
114	M-I NIGERIA LIMITED	Private Placement	January 17, 2007	40	40	Nil
				40	40	Nil
				40	40	Nil
				40	40	Nil

115	SCHLUMBERGER TESTING & PRODUCTION SERVICES LIMITED	Private Placement	January 17, 2007	36	36	Nil
				36	36	Nil
116	SEDCO FOREX OF NIGERIA LIMITED	Private Placement		36	36	Nil
				36	36	Nil
117	SOLUS SCHALL NIGERIA LIMITED	Private Placement	January 17, 2007	36	36	Nil
				36	36	Nil
				36	36	Nil
				36	36	Nil
118	LPG CALABAR DEPOT	Asset Sale	May 17, 2007	100	100	Nil
119	UNIPETRO (NOW OANDO PLC)	Core Investor Sale	May 2000	100	100	Nil
		Share Flotation	April 2001	100	100	Nil
120	AFRICAN PETROLEUM (AP)	Core Investor Sale	October 2000	100	100	Nil
		Share Flotation	May 2001	100	100	Nil
121	NATIONAL OIL AND CHEM. MARKETING CO. PLC (NOW CONOIL PLC)	Core Investor Sale	October 2000	75	75	Nil
		Share Flotation	April 2001	75	75	Nil
122	WEST AFRICAN REFINERY COMPANY LIMITED, SIERRA LEONE	Core Investor Sale	April 2004	72.6	72.66	Nil
123	ELEME PETROCHEMICALS COMPANY LIMITED (EPCL)	Core Investor Sale	December 2005	100	95	5
124	ABUJA ELECTRICITY DISTRIBUTION COMPANY PLC	Core Investor Sale	November 1, 2013	100	60	40

125	BENIN ELECTRICITY DISTRIBUTION COMPANY PLC	Core Investor Sale	November 1, 2013	100	60	40
126	EKO ELECTRICITY DISTRIBUTION COMPANY PLC	Core Investor Sale	November 1, 2013	100	60	40
127	ENUGU ELECTRICITY DISTRIBUTION COMPANY PLC	Core Investor Sale	November 1, 2013	100	60	40
128	IBADAN ELECTRICITY DISTRIBUTION COMPANY PLC	Core Investor Sale	November 1, 2013	100	60	40
129	IKEJA ELECTRICITY DISTRIBUTION COMPANY PLC	Core Investor Sale	November 1, 2013	100	60	40
130	JOS ELECTRICITY DISTRIBUTION COMPANY PLC	Core Investor Sale	November 1, 2013	100	60	40
131	KANO ELECTRICITY DISTRIBUTION COMPANY PLC	Core Investor Sale	November 1, 2013	100	60	40
132	PORT HARCOURT ELECTRICITY DISTRIBUTION COMPANY PLC	Core Investor Sale	November 1, 2013	100	60	40
133	YOLA ELECTRICITY DISTRIBUTION COMPANY PLC	Core Investor Sale	November 1, 2013	100	*60 (force majeure request under consider ation)*	40
134	SHIRORO POWER PLC	Concession	November 1, 2013	100	N/A	N/A
135	KAINJI POWER PLC	Concession	November 1, 2013	100	N/A	N/A
136	SAPELE POWER PLC	Core Investor Sale	November 1, 2013	100	100	Nil
137	GEREGU POWER PLC	Core Investor Sale	November 1, 2013	100	51	49
138	UGHELLI POWER PLC	Core Investor Sale	November 1, 2013	100	100	Nil
139	EGBIN POWER PLC	Core Investor Sale	November 1, 2013	100	70	30
140	OMOTOSHO POWER PLC	Debt/Equity Swap	January 26, 2015	100	100	Nil
141	OLORUNSOGO POWER PLC	Debt/Equity Swap	March5, 2014	100	100	Nil

146

| 142 | KADUNA ELECTRICITY DISC COY | Core Investor Sale | December 4, 2014 | 60 | 60 | 40 |
| 143 | NITEL/MTEL | Guided Liquidation | July 31, 2012 | 100 | N/A | 100 |

Source: Bureau of Public Enterprises Document, 2017.

APPENDIX B

List of Projects Scheduled For Concession under PPP by the Infrastructure Concession Regulatory Commission

S/N	PROJECTS & DESCRIPTION	MDA	SECTOR	PHASE	ESTIMATED COST OF PROJECT
1	Lagos to Ibadan express way. Reconstruction, rehabilitation and expansion work is in progress through traditional procurement. (contract to be funded by the federal government). The Infrastructure Bank Plc is assisting the Federal Government in raising funding to cover the Engineering procurement construction (EPC) funding gap	Federal ministry of power, works and Housing (FMPWH)	Roads	Procurement phase: The commission issued a full business case (FBC) compliance certificate for the Financing Arrangement	167,000,000,000 Naira
2	PPP development of dual carriage way from outer Northern express way (Murtala Mohammed way, Abuja) to ease congestion on Nyanya road and surrounding Axis	Federal Capital Development Authority (FCDA)	Roads	Development Phase: The ministry is to procure a TA to prepare an outline Business Case (OBC)	Not Available

3	PPPs for improved service delivery at the following:	Federal Ministry of Power, Works and Housing (FMPWH)	Roads	Development Phase: MDA to engage TA to prepare OBC	Not Available.
	Ilorin–Jebba–Mokwa–Tegina–Kaduna Road				
	Improvement of Apakun-Murtala Muhammed International Airport (MMA) Road route NO. F269				
	Phase 1: 2nd Lagos Outer Ring Road, Tin can Island-Igando-Lagos/Otta Road Interchange -Lagos/Ibadan Expressway				
	Phase 2: 2nd Lagos Outer Ring Road, Lekki-Ikorodu Shagamu/Benin Expressway				
	Abuja-Kaduna-Kano Dual Carriageway				
	Shagamu-Benin-Asaba Dual Carriageway				
	Onitsha-Enugu Dual Carriageway				
4	PPPs for improved service delivery at the following:	Federal Ministry of Power, Works & Housing (FMPWH)	Roads & Bridges	Development Phase: MDA to engage TA to prepare OBC	Not Available
	Enugu-Port Harcourt Road				

	Lagos-Iseyin-Kishi-Kaiama Road				
	Kaiama-Bahama-Kaoje-Gwambu-Fakku-Sokoto Road				
	Construction of a bridge over River Katsina Ala at Buruku, Benue State				
	Funtua-Zaria Road (A126)				
	GutoBagana Bridge over River Benue				
	Calabar-Odukpani-Itu-Ikot Ekpene Road				
5	Development of hydroelectric power from existing 10 small & medium dams across the country to generate about 45MW of off-grid power for the dam environments. These include Owena, Ikere Gorge and Oyan dams in Lot 1; Bakalori, Doma and Omi-Kampe dams in Lot 2; Challawa, Tiga, Jibiya and Zobe dams in Lot 3.	Federal Ministry of Power, Works &Housing (FMPWH)	Power	Procurement Phase: The Federal Executive Council approved the OBC of 6 projects on November 9, 2016. These include Ikere Gorge, Bakalori, Doma, Omi-Kampe, Jibiya and Zobe. These projects have now	29,356,876,605,23 Naira

				Moved to Procurement Phase where the Private Sector Project Proponent will be procured.	
6.	Operations and Maintenance of 30MW hydroelectric power from Gurara 1 multi-purpose dam, Kaduna State. The construction has been completed, while the evacuation facilities are almost completed.	Federal Ministry of Water Resources	Power	Development Phase: The Commissio n has issued OBC Compliance Certificate for FEC approval to be sought	6,679,288,975 Naira
7.	Concession of the Gurara 2 Greenfield multi-purpose Dam, Niger State. This includes 300MW of hydropower components of the dam.	Federal Ministry of Water Resources	Power, Agricultur e	Development Phase: MDA to engage TA to prepare OBC	Not Available
8.	Development of Tede Dam for Hydropower and other purposes.	Federal Ministry of Water Resources	Power, Agriculture	Development Phase: (Same as above)	Not Available
9.	Concession of Oturkpo Dam for Hydro power and other purposes.	Federal Ministry of Water Resources	Power, Agriculture	Development Phase: (Same as above)	Not Available
10.	Development of Dasin Hausa Dam for Hydro power	Federal Ministry of Water	Power, Agriculture	Development Phase: (Same as	Not Available

	and other purposes.	Resources		above)	
11.	Owena Multi-purpose Dam water supply.	Federal Ministry of Water Resources	Water Supply/ Agriculture	Development Phase: (Same as above)	Not Available
12.	Concession and leasing of grain storage facilities (33 silos across the country), to optimally operate and maintain the silos for an agreed period of time.	Federal Ministry of Agriculture and Rural Development	Agriculture	Development Phase: Technical review of OBC and Stakeholders consultation completed.	3,430,000,000 Naira
13.	Concession of:	Federal Ministry of Agriculture and Rural Development	Agriculture	Development Phase: MDA to engage TA to prepare OBC	Not Available
	Federal Coastal Fishery Terminal, Ebughu, Akwa Ibom State				
	Fish Processing Centre, Jebba, Kwara State				
	Agro Aviation Hangar, Kaduna				
14.	Operations and Maintenance of about 1000Ha irrigation infrastructure for commercial agriculture at Gurara 1 Dam, Azare-jere, Kaduna State to lease the irrigation facilities built by the Federal Government to private investors for optimal use.	Federal Ministry of Water Resources	Agriculture	Development Phase: OBC Certificate of Compliance issued.	N2,183,200,000.00

15.	Ibom Deep Seaport Project: An integrated, multi-purpose deep seaport which is being developed jointly by the FBN, Akwa Ibom State Government and subsequently, Private Investors. It is planned to be the deepest port in the West African sub-region.	Federal Ministry of Transportation /Akwa Ibom State Government	Ports	Procurement Phase: To Identify and engage a competent private sector project proponent	1,760,354,039 Dollars (836,168,168, 525 Naira) (This cost is being reviewed by the Ministry)
16.	Kirikiri Port Lighter Terminal 1 & 2: This proposes to procure a concessionaire to rehabilitate and upgrade the existing ports facility. The project development and procurement costs are being sponsored by the World Bank.	Federal Ministry of Transportation (FMoT)/Nigeri a Ports Authority (NPA)	Ports	Development Phase: OBC Compliance Certificate issued, for FEC approval	58.719,000,000
17.	Opereate and Manage Four River ports in the lower Niger mainly Onitsha, Lokoja, **Baro and** Oqula River Ports. Onitsha River port has been	Federal Ministry of Transportation (FMoT)/Natio nal Inland Waterways Authority (NIWA)	Ports	Development Phase: The commission has issued OBC Certificate for FEC approval to be sought	595,020,000 Naira

	selelcted as the pilot case. PPP Project development and procurement of the Inland port. Concession is being sponsored by the World Bank.				
18	Port Single Window: Introduction of electronic single window platform that can effectively coordinate all port related/cargo clearance activities capable of potentially transforming port operations by eliminating redundant procedures and duplications.	Federal Ministry of Transportation (FMoT)/NPA	Ports	Development Phase: MDA to engage TA to prepare OBC	Not Available
19	National Freight Intelligence and Transportation Hub (NAFITH): An application of information and communications technology in the management of transportation problems. It seeks to leverage on new innovation to provide needed solutions to the teething transport	Federal Ministry of Transportation (FMoT)/NPA	Ports	Development Phase: (Same as above)	Not Available

	problems in Apapa.				
20	Koko Port Concession: FGN to grant a new Concession over this port in 2017.	Federal Ministry of Transportation (FMoT)/NPA	Ports	Development Phase	Not Available
21	Ikorodu Lighter Terminal: The port is to salvage unclaimed or overtime containers in the ports, with a view to providing needed solutions to ports organisations and pave way to smoothen the new concessionaire's operations in the ports.	Federal Ministry of Transportation (FMoT)/NPA	Ports	Development Phase: MDA to engage TA to prepare OBC	Not Available
22	Provision of Utilities to the Ports: These include, but are not limited to the provisions of power and water.	Federal Ministry of Transportation (FMoT)/NPA	Ports	Development Phase: (Same as above)	Not Available
23	PPPs for Improved Service Delivery at the following facilities: Warri Dockyard Lokoja Dockyard	Federal Ministry of Transportation (FMoT)/NIWA	Ports	Development Phase: (Same as above)	Not Available

	Concession of AbamAma Jetty at Port Harcourt				
24	PPPs for Improved Service Delivery at the following facilites:	Federal Ministry of Transportation (FMoT)/NIWA	Ports	Development Phase: (Same as above)	Not Available
	Buoyage Vessels (B/V Anam at Onitsha)				
	Buoyage Vessels (B/V Bijiibo at Lokoja, Kogi State)				
	Buoyage Vessels (B/V Nembe at Lokoja, Kogi State)				
	Buoyage Vessels (B/V Numan at Lokoja, Kogi State)				
25	PPPs for Improved Service Delivery at the following facilities:	Federal Ministry of Transportation (FMoT)/NIWA	Ports	Development Phase: (Same as above)	Not Available
	Motor Ferry (M/F Calabar at Lokoja, Kogi State)				
	Motor Ferry (M/F EffiatMbo at Lokoja, KogiStae)				
	Motor Ferry (M/F Donga at Makurdi, Benue State)				
	Water Bus (W/B at Yauri, Kebbi State)				

	3 Nos. 40-45 Passenger Sitter Ferries at Lokoja, Kogi State				
	Water Hyacinth Clearing Equipment (Water Master Classic III at Onitsha)				
	2 Nos. 40-45 Passenger Sitter Ferries at Lagos				
26	PPPs for improved service delivery at the following facilities:	Federal Ministry of Transportation (FMoT)/NIWA	Ports	Development Phase: (Same as above)	Not Available
	Marina Jetty at Lagos				
	Apapa Jetty at Lagos				
	Oyingbo Jetty at Lagos				
	Maraoko Jetty at Lagos				
	Abayomi Drive Jetty at Lagos				
	Osborne Jetty at Lagos				
	Calabar Jetty at Calabar				
27	The Dagbolu Inland Container Depot (ICD) project concerns the development of a Greenfield ICD in Ogun State, South-West Nigeria.	Federal Ministry of Transportation (FMoT)/Nigeria Shippers Council (NSC)	Inland Port	Development Phase: The Commission has issued OBC Compliance Certificate for FEC approval to be sought	1,072,480,000 Naira

	The ICD is being developed to exploit the strategic advantages in Nigeria's huge export and import markers by making the country a trans-shipment hub for the West African sub-region.				
28	Development of Container Freight Depot (CFD) in Oqwasi-Uku, Delta State: This has a design that consists of an annual 5000 TEUs capacity facility which can be expanded with increasing throughput	Federal Ministry of Transportation (FMoT)/NSC	Inland Port	Development Phase: This is an Unsolicited Proposal. The procurement of a TA is in progress	
29	Development of Inland Container Depot (ICD) in Onitsha, Anambra State: This has a design that consists of an annual 5000 TUEs capacity facility which can be expanded with increasing throughput.	Federal Ministry of Transportation (FMoT)/NSC	Inland Port	Development Phase: The Procurement of a Transaction Adviser has commenced	920,000,000 Naira
30	PPP Development of an Inland Container Depot (ICD) in Lolo, Kebbi State. Outline business	Federal Ministry of Transportation (FMoT)/NSC	Inland Port	Development Phase: Unsolicited proposal reviewed by ICRC,	Not Available

	case (OBC) received from the Nigeria Shippers Council (NSC) in respect of the Unsolicited proposal developed by Deltatlantic Nigeria Ltd.			awaiting submission of revised OBC by MDA	
31	Development of Inland Container Depot (ICD) in Nnewi, Anambra State.	Federal Ministry of Transportation (FMoT)/NSC	Inland Port	Development Phase: The OBC was reviewed by ICRC and comments sent to NSC for revision	Not Available
32	Development of Inland Container Depot (ICD) in Benin, Edo State.	Federal Ministry of Transportation (FMoT)/NSC	Inland Port	Development Phase: OBC reviewed and returned NSC	Not Available
33	Development of Truck Transit Park (TTP) in Obollo-Afor, Enugu State	Federal Ministry of Transportation (FMoT)/NSC	Inland Port	Development Phase: NDA to engage TA to prepare OBC	Not Available
34	Development of Truck Transit Park (TTP) in Lokoja, Kogi State	Federal Ministry of Transportation (FMoT)/NSC	Inland Port	Development Phase: (Same as above)	Not Available
35	PPP Development of Abuja Mass Transit Rail Lot 1A and 3 Projects for the FCTA in Abuja. Provision of rolling stock, additional stations, maintenance	Federal Capital Territory Administration (FCTA)	Rail	Development Phase: OBC to be resubmitted to the commission	32,647,000,000 Naira

	depot and operation of the system.				
36	Concession of the narrow guage:	Federal Ministry of Transportation (FMoT)/NRC	Rail	Development Phase: An OBC has been submitted by GE and Government, and its Advisory team are reviewing the document	2,000,000,000 us Dollars 950,000,000,000 Naira
	Eastern Railway (Port Harcourt to Maiduguri)				
	Western (Lagos to Kano) Railway lines in the country				
	FGN is considering an Unsolicited proposal submitted by General Electrics to have a concession over the Western and Eastern Rail lines. The Nigeria Infrastructure Advisory Facility (NIAF), and arm of the United Kingdom Department for International Development (DFID), had also assisted the FGN in funding the preparation of an Outline Business Case (OBC) as part of the project development work for the concession of the railway lines.				

37	Lagos – Shagamu – Ijebu Ode – Ore – Benin City (300KM) (Standard guage).	Federal Ministry of Transportation (FMoT)/ Nigerian Railway Corporation (NRC)	Rail	Development Phase: OBCs are being prepared	Not Available
	Benin – Agbor– OgwashiUku – Asaba – Onitsha – Nnewi – Owerri – Aba with additional line from Onitsha – Enugu – Abakaliki (500km) (Standard Guage)				
	Ajaokuta (Eganyi) -Obajana – Jakura – Baro – Abuja with additional line from Ajaokuta to Oturkpo (533km) (Standard Guage)				
	Zaria – Funtua – Tsafe – Gusau – Kaura – Namoda – Sokoto – Illela – Birninkoni (520km) (Standard Guage)				
	Lagos – Ibadan – Oshogbo – Baro – Abuja (615KM) (High speed)				
38	PPP Development of Abuja Light Rail Lot 2 Network route. The distance will cover 54.1 kilo meters from Garki Area 11 passing through the Interchange	Federal Capital Territory Administration (FCTA)	Rail	Development Phase: TA yet to be appointed.	Not Available

	centre at Eagle Square to Gudu, Nyanya, Karu axis, in Abuja.				
39	Rehabilitation, Management and Operation of the National Trade and International Business Centre, Lagos (NTIBC)	Federal Ministry of Trade & Investment/Ta fawa Balewa Square Management Board (TBSMB)	Trade & Investment	Development Phase: TA has been procured and is currently preparing an OBC	31,000,000,000 Naira
40	Establishment of the Mechanic's villages to stimulate the growth and development of the mechanic busi ness in a specialized and orderly manner.	Federal Ministry of Trade & Investment/Na tional Automotive Council (NAC)	Trade & Investment	Development Phase: The OBC has been reviewed by ICRC and comments sent to NAC for revision and submission	5,300,000,000
41	Development of 23 Industrial Development Clusters (IDCs) in 6 geopolitical zones.	Federal Ministry of Trade and Investment/ Small and Media Enterprises Development Agency of Nigeria (SMEDAN)	Trade & Investment	Development Phase: Technical Committee to submit feasibility report.	Not Available
42	Development for New Eko Project/Lagoon City, Lagos: An Unsolicited proposal for the sand-filling and reclamation of	Federal Ministry of Power, Works and Housing (FMPW&H)	Social/ Urban Infrastructur e (Housing)	Development Phase: An OBC is being developed	Not Available

	water bodies within the vicinity of existing Banana Island, Lagos.				
43	Marina Quayside Strip Development Project: A transformative urban/waterfront Project along the Marina axis in Lagos. It is intended to be a tourism centre that wouldprovide hotels, condominiums, commercial complexes, recreation facilities, bus transport terminals, offices and residential buildings.	Federal Ministry of Power, Works and Housing (FMPW&H)	Social/Urban Infrastructure (Housing)	Development Phase: The OBC was reviewed by ICRC and comments sent to MDA for revision.	Not Available
44	Ship building yard with breaking, recycling technology and wreck identification and removal.	Federal Ministry of Transportation (FMoT)/ Nigerian Maritime Administration and Safety Agency (NIMASA)	Maritime	Development Phase: MDA to engage TA to prepare OBC	Not Available
45	Management and operations of the modulation/floating dry dock (outsourcing).	Federal Ministry of Transportation (FMoT)/ Nigerian Maritime Administration	Maritime	Development Phase: (Same as above)	Not Available

		and Safety Agency (NIMASA)			
46	Procurement of operational vessels, maritime patrol aircraft, coordination/surveillance centre and other operational equipment (Finance lease)	Federal Ministry of Transportation (FMoT)/ Nigerian Maritime Administration and Safety Agency (NIMASA)	Maritime	Development Phase: (Same as above)	Not Available
47	Outsourcing of NIMASA's Training Centre and Guest House at Nigerian Maritime Resource Development Centre (NMRDC), Kirikiri, Lagos State.	Federal Ministry of Transportation (FMoT)/ Nigerian Maritime Administration and Safety Agency (NIMASA)	Maritime	Development Phase: (Same as above)	Not Available
48	PPPs to develop a Multilevel car park at NIMASA Headquarters	Federal Ministry of Transportation (FMoT)/ Nigerian Maritime Administration and Safety Agency (NIMASA)	Maritime	Development Phase: (Same as above)	Not Available
49	Unsolicited proposal for development of platform for pollution	Federal Ministry of Transportation (FMoT)/ Nigerian Maritime Administration and Safety Agency (NIMASA)	Maritime	Development Phase: (Same as above)	Not Available

50	Verification gross mass imo solar – safety of life at sea	Federal Ministry of Transportation (FMoT)/ Nigerian Maritime Administration and Safety Agency (NIMASA)	Maritime	Development Phase: (Same as above)	Not Available
51	Concession of 4 International Airports (Abuja, Lagos, Kano and Port Harcourt)	Federal Ministry of Transportation (FMoT)	Aviation	Development Phase: (Same as above)	Not Available
52	Establishment of a Maintenance, Repair and overhaul (MRO) centre	Federal Ministry of Transportation (FMoT)	Aviation	Development Phase: (Same as above)	Not Available
	Development of Aerotropolis (Airport City)				
	Development of Cargo/Agro-allied airport terminals				
53	Production and Management of Nigeria's e– passport project, Production of International Civil Aviation Organisation (ICAO) compliant E-passpport.	Federal Ministry of Interior	Immigration	Development Phase: OBC to be updated by project proponent.	Not Available
54	Procure new correctional facilities in three (3) locations in Nigeria on a land (Valley) swap basis at Lagos, Owerri and Kaduna.	Federal Ministry of Interior/ Nigerian Prison Service	Prisons	Development Phase: MDA to engage TA to prepare OBC	Not Available

55	Prison Integrated Farm Facility at Ozala (Edo State), Kujama (Kaduna State) and Lakushi (Plateau State)	Federal Ministry of Interior/ Nigerian Prison Service	Prisons	Development Phase: A preferred bidder has emerged as TA and negotiations are under way	Not Available
	Refurbishment of Existing laundry facility in Kuje and establishment of Industrial laundry facility in other prison locations nationwide				
	Construction of Prison Officers homes at various locations in Nigeria				
	The Aba shoe project, for production of Made In Nigeria products				
56	PPPs to develop the following projects:	Federal Ministry of Interior/ Nigerian Priso n Service	National Security	Development Phase: MDA to engage TA to prepare OBC	Not Available
	Passengers Information System				
	ECOWAS Biometric Identification System				
	Information Verification System				
	Security Guards Biometric Data Collection, verification and authentic system				

166

57	Construction of an ultramodern forensic laboratory at the Police Headquarters Building in Abuja.	Federal Ministry of Interior	Security	Development Phase: MDA to engage TA to prepare OBC	Not Available
58	Renovation and refurbishment of the Obalende & Falomo Police Barracks in Lagos.	Federal Ministry of Interior	Security	Development Phase: (Same as above)	Not Available
59	Establishment of selected weapons and military equipment assembly lines	Defence Industries Corporation of Nigeria	Security	Development Phase: (Same as above)	Not Available
	Establishment of Mobile Solar Powered Generating sets				
	Production of Ballistic Vests and procurement of Raw Materials				
60	Construction of staff housing estate, shopping complex and new House Officers' (Doctors)'quarters	Federal Ministry of Health/ University of Port Harcourt teaching Hospital	Health	Development Phase: Procurement of TA has commenced	9,000,000,00 0 Naira
61	Development of a Tertiary Medical facility (Abuja Medical Mall/City) on a greenfield site in Abuja to harness the potential of the private health sector and provide high quality alternatives to Nigerians who require specialist	Federal Ministry of Health	Health	Development Phase: MDA to engage TA to prepare OBC	Not Available

	medical care in the country.			
62	Management of the Warehouse in a box project (Lagos and Abuja). For refrigeration of vaccines and subsequent distribution to needed locations.	Federal Ministry of Health	Health	Development Phase: Inception report has been submitted by TA	Not Available
63	Increase of financial inclusion (FI) penetration rate in the country by providing banking services to the financially excluded population through NIPOST offices nationwide.	Federal Ministry of Communication Technology /NIPOST	ICT	Development Phase: MDA to engage TA to prepare OBC	Not Available
64	Pedestrian Metal barriers on municipal roads: The project is for the repair and replacement of damaged sections. This will also involve the development of new areas of expansion for the erection of new metal barriers within the Municipal area.	Federal Capital Development Authority (FCDA)	Social/ Urban Infrastructure	Development Phase: (Same as above)	Not Available
65	Construction of Automated Parking Centres in	Federal Capital Development Authority (FCDA)	Social/ Urban Infrastructure	Development Phase: (Same as above)	Not Available

	designated car parks in the Federal Capital Territory.				
66	PPP to develop corporate head office of Federal Housing Authority (FHA) in Abuja located at the Central Business District of Abuja.	Federal Housing Authority (FHA)	Housing	Development Phase: (Same as above)	Not Available
67	Development of new towns in Abuja at Kwali and Bwari Area Councils	Federal Housing Authority (FHA)	Housing	Development Phase: (Same as above)	Not Available
68	Upgrading/ Rebuilding of National Stadium, Lagos. Completion of athletics' hostel, Abuja	Federal Ministry of Youths and Sports	Sports	Development Phase: Ministry seeking TA services	Not Available
69	Construction of Council for the Regulation of Engineering in Nigeria (COREN) head office complex in Abuja	Council for the Regulation of Engineering in Nigeria	Housing	Development Phase: MDA to engage TA to prepare OBC	Not Available
70	Upgrade of the ICT laboratories/busines s centres in Federal schools	Federal Ministry of Education	Education	Development Phase: (Same as above)	Not Available
	Upgrade of existing libraries				
	Upgrade of vocational schools				

71	Development of an International Conference Centre	National Mathematical Centre	Education	Development Phase: (Same as above)	Not Available
	Construction of National Mathematical Centre – International Science Academy (NMC-IMSA)				
72	Proposed construction of student'shostels, 500-units of staff housing, roads and drainages, staff/students cafeteria, bio gas Electricity powered plant and Poultry farm	Federal Ministry of Education	Education	Development Phase: (Same as above)	Not Available
73	Online applicatio n system for E-registration platform, Computation/ compilation of students result, e-learning and web portal development	Federal Ministry of Education	Education	Development Phase: (Same as above)	Not Available
74	Proposed construction of Vice Chancellor's Lodge, Principal Officers' Quarters, Senior Staff Housing, Junior Staff Housing, External Electrification. Borehole and Overhead Tanks, etc.	Federal Ministry of Education	Education	Development Phase: (Same as above)	Not Available
75	PPPs to develop the following projects:	Federal Ministry of Environment	Environment	Development Phase: (Same as above)	Not Available

	Waste to Wealth management (recycling) including scrap metal plant.				
	Solid waste management				
	Completion of Bamboo processing machine (Livelihood enhancement) through bamboo value – chain development, Lokoja. Kogi State.				
	Completion of renovation of structures and equipment at Forest Utilization Centre, Benin City				
76	Establishment of Federal Ministry of Environment's clean and green campaign to end open dedication in public areas by 2019, by providing public toilets nationwide. Pilots to be in FCT public schools, m otor parks and market places, and extended to 36 states.	Federal Ministry of Environment	Environment	Development Phase: (Same as above)	Not Available

	Framework for Plastic Industry and other private sector companies to take plastic waste off streets by 2019				
77	Development of a new Head Office for the Federal Ministry of Environment (to be completed in 2018)	Federal Ministry of Environment	Environment	Development Phase: (Same as above)	Not Available

Source: Infrastructure Concession and Regulatory Commission Publication, 2017.

INDEX

A

Abacha, Sani 24
Adeosun, Kemi 51, 75, 133, 137
African Continental Bank 14
Ake, Calude 12, 14, 34, 133
ANAMCO 14
Antitrust and competition laws 69
Anyim, Pius iv
Awka blacksmiths 12

B

Babangida, Ibrahim 16, 114
Benin bronze casts 12
Bi Courtney 30, 31
British Petroleum 15
Budget Office 68
Buhari, Mohammadu 43
Bureau of Public Enterprises iv, 19, 67,
70, 90, 110, 147
Bureau of Public Procurement ... 39, 68

C

Central Bank of Nigeria 44, 48, 62, 75,
103, 104
Civil Aeronautics Board 54
Civil Society and the Media 65
Class structure of a society 34
Concession 20, 23, 24, 25, 26, 27, 28,
29, 30, 31, 38, 39, 41, 42, 59, 70, 71, 79,
80, 110, 133, 160
Consumer Protection Council 94
Corporate Affairs Commission 96
Council of Registered Builders of
Nigeria 119

D

Dangote, Aliko 68
Debt Management Office 68
Distribution companies (DISCOS) . 21

E

Eastern Nigeria 11
Economic Community for West
African States 111
Economic Deregulation Committee 87
Economic Management
Implementation Team 69
Economic Stabilization (Temporary
Provisions) Act in 1982 16
Elumelu, Tony 68
Energy Commission of Nigeria 111,
112
Engels, Fredrich 34

F

Federal Capital Territory 76, 159, 161,
168
Federal Communications Commission
.... 54
Federal Inland Revenue Service 67
Federal Power Commission 54
Federal Trade Commission 54
Financial Reporting Council of Nigeria
.... 53
First Bank 18, 46
Fiscal Responsibility Commission .. 43,
47, 56, 57, 66
Fourth National Development Plan,
1981-1985 14

G

Generation companies, (GENCOS) 21
Ghana 49, 52, 133
Goldie, Georgie 12

I

Igbo-Ukwu bronze casts 12
Industrial Deregulation Committee. 87
Infrastructure Concession Regulatory
Commission. iv, 24, 40, 46, 61, 80, 137

Interstate Commerce Commission. 54, 55

J

John Holt 14
Joint Admission and Matriculation Board, JAMB 99
Jonathan, Goodluckiv, 52, 53, 67, 68, 69, 133, 135

K

Kano cloth weaving 12
Kyari, Abba 43

L

Lagos-Ibadan expressway 30
Lever Brothers 14

M

Manufacturers Association of Nigeria 67
Marx, Karl 33, 34, 135
Marxist political economy.... 35, 36, 37
Medical Laboratory Science Council of Nigeria 66, 67
Meeting on Regulatory Reform 87
MTN 43, 53, 62, 136, 137
Murtala/Obasanjo military regime .. 15

N

National Assembly61, 70, 80, 86, 88, 92, 106, 132
National Association of Chambers of Industry, Mines and Agriculture 65
National Automotive Council..78, 162
National Bio-safety Management Agency Act 2015 93
National Broadcasting Commission40, 123
National Council on Privatization ... 19
National Economic Reconstruction Fund 74

National Human Rights Commission of Nigeria 113
National Lottery Regulatory Commission 106
National Mass Communication Policy 123
National Park Service 93
National Procurement Council 64
NEPA 14
Nigeria Bar Association 65
Nigeria Communications Commission 39, 62
Nigeria Copyright Commission 113
Nigeria Electricity Regulatory Commission 39, 42
Nigeria Football Federation 107
Nigeria National Petroleum Corporation 52
Nigeria Nuclear Regulatory Authority 39, 117
Nigeria Ports Authority.... 90, 110, 153
Nigeria Shippers Council89, 110, 157, 158
Nigeria Society of Engineers 65
Nigeria Stock Exchange 17
Nigerian bourgeoisie 22
Nigerian Broadcasting Commission 60
Nigerian Maritime Administration and Safety Agency 163, 164, 165
Nigerian Maritime Administration and Safety Agency (NIMASA) 108
Nigerian Press Council 123
NITEL 14, 19, 39, 147
Nnoli, Okwudiba 11, 135
Nok terracotta 12
Nursing Council of Nigeria 127

O

Obama, Barrack 55
Ojukwu, Sir Louis Odumegwu 14
Okonjo-Iweala, Ngozi 67, 68
Oshita, Oshita v
Osinbajo, Yemi 56, 136

Ovia, Jim 68

P

PAN 14, 140
Partial commercialization 18
Paterson Zochonis 14
Pension Commission 39, 44
Power Holding Company of Nigeria 21
Presidential Commission on Administrative Reform 87, 136
Public Enterprises (Privatization and Commercialization) Decree of 1998 20
Public-Private Partnership 25

R

Radiographers Registration Board of Nigeria 127
Regulatory institutions 38, 39, 40, 41, 42, 45, 46, 47, 50, 52, 53, 54, 55, 57, 59, 60, 61, 62, 63, 64, 65, 66, 67, 77, 81, 82, 84, 89, 91
Royal Niger Company 12

S

Salaries, Incomes and Wages Commission 47
Sanusi, Sanusi Lamido 46
Securities and Exchange Commission 49, 68, 70, 103
Security and Exchange Commission 40, 48, 53

Shagari, Shehu 16
Small and Medium Enterprises Development Agency, SMEDAN ... 74
Soludo, Charles C 37, 52, 137
South Korea 86, 88
Special Purpose Vehicle 30
Stock Exchange 14, 48
Suleiman. v
Supreme Court 56

T

Technical Committee on Privatization and Commercialization 18
Trans-Atlantic trades 12
Trans-Sahara trades 12
Traore, Karim ii

U

United African Company 14
United Kingdom 13, 160
United Nations General Assembly 113
United States 46, 54, 55

V

Viability Gap Financing 28

Y

Yar'Adua, Umaru 31, 52, 138

Z

Zenith Bank 46, 68

www.ingramcontent.com/pod-product-compliance
Lightning Source LLC
Chambersburg PA
CBHW071350280326
41927CB00040B/2642